This book is such a treasure! We spend a lot of time talking about how marriage takes work and parenting takes work, but we sort of expect friendships to just appear in our lives and sail on for the long haul. But that's not how my life and friendships have gone, and I'm so grateful for Laura's willingness to open an honest conversation about how to make friends, what kinds of friends we need, and how to be a good friend. I love Laura's writing, and her wisdom and wit sparkle on every page. When you finish this book, you'll want to reach out to every friend in your life, and you'll have the skills and perspective to make a few new ones, too.

Shauna Niequist, *New York Times* bestselling
author of *I Guess I Haven't Learned That Yet*

She already taught us the importance of sharing our stuff and was brave enough to go first. Now, Laura Tremaine shows up for us again, this time bringing hard-won wisdom, honest confessions, and a thoughtful new vocabulary for how to talk about being friends (especially for those of us who secretly worry we're bad ones). Finally, a useful friendship book for grownups.

Emily P. Freeman, *Wall Street Journal*
bestselling author of *The Next Right Thing*

A lot of women think that if we're not going on vacation with a montage-worthy bestie, we're doing friendship wrong. In *The Life Council*, Laura Tremaine candidly and compassionately tells us the truth about the beauty and vastness of adult friendship, offering a relational framework that women deeply crave. No longer are we stuck in a restrictive paradigm of what it means to make and keep friends. *The Life Council* teaches us to paint a new picture of friendship, one with more color and texture than we realized was possible.

Kendra Adachi, *New York Times*
bestselling author of *The Lazy Genius*
Way and *The Lazy Genius Kitchen*

The Life Council

10 Friends Every Woman Needs

LAURA TREMAINE

ZONDERVAN
BOOKS

ZONDERVAN BOOKS

The Life Council
Copyright © 2023 by Laura Tremaine

Requests for information should be addressed to:
Zondervan, *3900 Sparks Dr. SE, Grand Rapids, Michigan 49546*

Zondervan titles may be purchased in bulk for educational, business, fundraising, or sales promotional use. For information, please email SpecialMarkets@Zondervan.com.

ISBN 978-0-310-35998-2 (audio)

Library of Congress Cataloging-in-Publication Data

Names: Tremaine, Laura, 1979- author.
Title: The life council: 10 friends every woman needs / Laura Tremaine.
Description: Grand Rapids: Zondervan, 2023. | Summary: "In The Life Council, author and podcaster Laura Tremaine offers women a new way to think about friendships and practical ways to find, build, and keep the right friend for every season of their lives"—Provided by publisher.
Identifiers: LCCN 2022054484 (print) | LCCN 2022054485 (ebook) | ISBN 9780310359951 (trade paperback) | ISBN 9780310367277 (hardcover) | ISBN 9780310359968 (ebook)
Subjects: LCSH: Female friendship. | Friendship. | BISAC: FAMILY & RELATIONSHIPS / Friendship
Classification: LCC HM1161 .T74 2023 (print) | LCC HM1161 (ebook) | DDC 302.34082—dc23/eng/20221222
LC record available at https://lccn.loc.gov/2022054484
LC ebook record available at https://lccn.loc.gov/2022054485

Any internet addresses (websites, blogs, etc.) and telephone numbers in this book are offered as a resource. They are not intended in any way to be or imply an endorsement by Zondervan, nor does Zondervan vouch for the content of these sites and numbers for the life of this book.

The author is represented by the literary agency of Alive Literary Agency, www.aliveliterary.com.

Names and identifying characteristics of some individuals have been changed to preserve their privacy.

Poem by David Gate used with permission.

Cover design: Faceout Studio / Jeff Miller
Cover illustrations: mini cherry studio / OoddySmile Studio / Shutterstock
Interior design: Sara Colley

Printed in the United States of America

---

23 24 25 26 27 LBC 5 4 3 2 1

*For my Life Council members currently
serving lifetime appointments:*

*Kimi Dallman
Andy Duty
Jaime Hammer
Lindsay Lawler
Cara Pence
and Meg Tietz*

Be kind about the names
Your friends give to their children
Praise their haircuts
Love their tattoos
It doesn't really matter
If that's what you would do
Like every selfie
All of them
Clap their songs
Cheer them on
You were born with a limitless
Supply of encouragements
Use every one of them
Don't wait for the eulogies
To speak out loud
That your friends are precious
And they make you feel proud.

—DAVID GATE

Contents

PART I

The Most Important Relationship

A Friendship Reckoning

We were almost a year into the COVID-19 pandemic as I stood in my backyard, carefully spacing two lounge chairs six feet apart. I placed a patterned blanket on the ground and loaded it with two small trays of snacks. It was dark outside already, so I added candles to the blanket, making the whole scene feel more like a date night than a friendship reckoning.

Officially, we were meeting because I had hurt her feelings in a group text the week before. But we both knew the coming conversation was bigger than that.

At first, I hadn't realized how much the casual exchange had stung my friend, but then again, intention and tone are often misread in text. The social isolation of the Los Angeles lockdown made all of our friendship communications a little heightened, and the fact that the misunderstanding was going down in front of others—on the screens of our mom friends across the city—also added to the drama.

But if it had just been about my dismissive text, we

probably would have patched things up pretty quickly. We know each other well, and we're generally understanding about what can be misconstrued when typing quickly into a group conversation while also multitasking.

Still, it took me a few days before I realized that the text conflict needed more than a quick apology. The surface of the discord was about me being cavalier about her valid COVID concerns. The deeper tangle stemmed from my friend's perception that I never kept her perspective in mind. That I never tried to see anything through her lens. That I imposed my own point of view onto everything and everyone, even when our life circumstances were wildly different.

It's true: I can be selfish in relationships. I was already a little bruised from two other recent friend conflicts in which, again, I was the one who had misstepped and had to make things right with women I loved. I had committed the same friendship felony with each: I had failed to respond to their messages. I had ghosted their texts, calls, and voicemails without explanation, and these were not just routine check-ins. One was doing me a massive favor and needed some feedback, and the other was caring for a sick parent and could have used some support. Both of those friends were direct with me about my transgressions, so I couldn't dismiss them or claim they were being high-maintenance. Nope, it was me. I had neglected them and our friendship. I had ceased communicating when that was the thing most required. Then I had blissfully assumed we'd high-five and all would be forgiven (I mean, they knew me, right? I'm flaky sometimes!) but was taken aback when both women, separately, had demanded that I change my behavior.

Those two friendships had mended (because they do know

me and believed my sincere apologies), but I had been licking my wounds for a few months, alternately beating myself up and giving myself grace about all the ways I had failed as a friend in my lifetime. A dramatic response, yes, but it had been eye-opening in the same way that everything in that first year of the pandemic was eye-opening, including our friendships. We were suddenly intensely aware of our own mortality and how quickly the world can change and which relationships matter the most.

So when that group text went sideways, I inwardly groaned. Another friendship lesson? Hadn't I been hit over the head with this enough? My indignation gave way to a deeper fear: *maybe I **was** a bad friend.*

I lit the candles and grabbed blankets against the chilly night just a few moments before my friend walked quietly through the back gate. She wouldn't have knocked or otherwise announced her presence if she was coming in the kitchen door, either. There was never a need. We were that close.

She had her long hair back in a high ponytail, and big, chunky jewelry accessorized her tank top and black overalls. I was embracing the loungewear look of the lockdown and had just barely gussied up the yoga-pants-and-brightly-colored-hoodie combo that had become my daily uniform. We didn't hug hello. Because of the virus, we hadn't hugged in a long time. Physical affection was another thing the pandemic had stolen from us.

We chatted awkwardly at first, about our kids and some dumb pop culture news. She had brought her own drink and blanket, and for the first few minutes, she held them both tightly to her chest. We started to settle into our chairs, and she grinned broadly at the props and scenery I'd staged in my attempt to create a cozy reverence for this conversation. This broke the ice as we both giggled at the things I had grabbed from the house to adorn the space between our chairs. The truth was, I think that little tableau said a lot about how I wanted the night to go. It showed that I was honoring both her and us. Our friendship was only a few years old, yet it had already forged some of my greatest memories. On that night, I was trying to make up for being flippant about her feelings by going overboard with care for the reconciliation.

The tone I set in the backyard that night might have been sweet, or it might have been weird, but ultimately, it worked. Our long conversation was stilted at first, then grew more heated before we had each finally said enough words to make the other understand our side a little better. When she slipped back through the gate a few hours later to her car in the driveway, things weren't perfect, but we were still friends.

It could have gone either way. Later, we confessed to one another that we had braced ourselves for the friendship to end that night. Not because of an errant text, but because of the dozens of tiny slights that had built up into a mountain that could have felt insurmountable. Did my friend and I ever intend for hurt feelings to become so serious? Of course not. And I believe now that we never would have had such a buildup of tension or an obvious misunderstanding if we had been seeing one another in person all along. Communicating solely through a screen for so long impacted our natural rhythm and ability to intuit each other's intentions. In the days leading up to that night, I had crafted an intricate defense for myself in my head, but all of that melted away when I saw her walk through my backyard in person. Yes, we needed to hash out our differences in a hard conversation and offer apologies, but more importantly, we needed to feel the energy of the friend-ship together to be reminded of its meaning and how much we wanted it to continue. We could have ended something that is a joy for both of us. It happens. But I'm so glad we didn't.

These fraught friendship experiences of the last few years made me feel ill-equipped to write this book. But those same conflicts also made me dig deeper into the friendships that sustain me now and to think back on those that have shaped my life. Because I credit my friendships—from the decades-long sisterhoods to the fleeting and seasonal sidekicks—with having influence over my confidence, my favorite memories, my style and taste, my career choices, and even my motherhood.

Yet adult friendship isn't talked about with much nuance. We use the term "friend" to cover a wide swath of relation-ships in our life, from those who are barely more than an acquaintance to those who would answer our call in the middle of the night. How do those two people deserve the same title? It's not that we don't classify them at all—we understand the difference between best friends and everyone else. But we don't have more specific terminology for the plethora of people in our lives who fall under the large umbrella of "friend."

At least I didn't until I was introduced to the idea of having a Life Council—an advisory board of friends much like a business or organization has an advisory board of professionals—by my friend Chris Ann over ten years ago during a retreat I hosted at my lake house. As Chris Ann was explaining the concept, we were sitting in a circle of women who had met on the internet and who I had invited to my home after months of chatting in a Facebook group. A weekend of internet-strangers-turned-friends felt like a risk, but this particular group came together online at a time in my life when I was at my loneliest, and their friendship (even through a screen) was a life raft for me when I was drowning in early motherhood. While certain interests drew us together initially, we encompassed a wide range of ages, lifestyles, and personalities, so when Chris Ann suggested that we were all members of one another's Life Councils, the idea made sense.

Chris Ann doesn't remember exactly where she heard about the theory of a Life Council, but it's clear the idea of surrounding yourself with a committee of sorts has been in the zeitgeist for a while. Oprah Winfrey has talked about having a personal advisory board of people you can trust to help you make big decisions, with an emphasis on friends who have your best interests in mind and not their own. Bestselling author Bruce Feiler wrote a 2010 memoir called *Council of Dads* about the men who might become father figures to his young daughters after he was diagnosed with bone cancer. And in the rising trend of professional entrepreneur groups, collecting mentors and comrades has been touted as a strong way to succeed in business.

WE'RE MORE CONNECTED TO EVERYONE WE'VE EVER MET THANKS TO THE INTERNET, AND YET WE'RE LONELIER THAN EVER.

Personally, while I liked the concept of a Life Council, at first it seemed almost juvenile to categorize friends in this way. I didn't want to rank the people I cared about. I didn't want to formalize an inner circle of friends in such a way that would leave others out. I resonated with *Untamed* author Glennon Doyle's image of a friendship horseshoe: open and not closed, ever-widening.

Still, over the last few years, I couldn't escape the research that tells us we're more connected to everyone we've ever met thanks to the internet, and yet we're lonelier than ever. How are we to bridge that gap between having (literally) a million options for friendship and the fact that many of us can't seem to make or maintain that elusive "best friend" or "friend group"?

My relationship blunders over the last few years made me take a step back and consider what matters about my friendships and what type of friend I wanted to be. It also required that I think honestly about how different people fit into my life, schedule, and heart, which felt a bit awkward. I turned to the Life Council framework as a way to classify the different types of women who have shaped me and to see my relationships from a place of gratitude for what they are without trying to fit every female friendship into the mold of what culture tells me friendship should look like.

When I began to understand the roles of certain friends—including the role I play in their lives as well—I found acceptance for these different flavors of friendships in my past, present, and future. It allowed me to let go of some disappointments and sadness and gave me real hope for the friendships to come. After my friendship reckoning of 2020, I vowed to put effort into and attention towards these relationships that are continually teaching me how I want to walk in the world.

My friends are among the greatest joys of my life. I don't take them for granted, because I've been through the lonely years. I don't live in the naivete that all friendships last forever, because I've been through loss. I do carry the responsibility that my friendships deserve because I now understand that it's often more work than we acknowledge. Long before I gave any of them a title on my Life Council, I was made better by having these women in my life.

This book is about the work and joy of friendship. Our culture gives a lot of attention to other relationships in our adult lives, like marriage and parenthood and healthy boundaries in the workplace or with in-laws, and we're led to believe that friendships should be easy, that they should be fun in the good times and helpful in the hard times and that they should just show up naturally.

But no one really tells us how to make friends, or release friends, or how to think about friendship when it gets complicated. Making friends isn't easy or natural for all of us. Friendship breakups are treated like melodrama instead of heartbreak. There are no rule books for how to handle a friendship that has layers of good and bad.

I'm only a friendship expert on my own friendships, much like you're an expert on your own friendships, but I've spent years writing and talking about this online. This book comes from hundreds of hours of discussions on social media, recorded on my podcast, and from my own life, and I want this book to be an extension of those conversations.

In these pages, we're going to talk about giving our friendships the reverence they deserve and how to take a step back and look at them as an important aspect of a wholehearted life. We're going to acknowledge the pain that comes when friendships end, and we're going to open our eyes to the freedom that a good friendship offers. But while I will lay out for you my friendship philosophies and the Life Council I've assembled for myself, these thoughts are not prescriptive. It's meant to be a conversation starter in your own life, or in your own journal, or with your own friends—an interactive conversation in book form.

I hope it makes you think about your past and present friendships in a new way, and that it inspires more connection. When you're done reading *The Life Council*, I hope you feel more equipped to serve, love, and enjoy your friendships, whatever their number.

A Personal History
of Friendship

couldn't explain my Life Council to you without sharing
a brief history of my own friendships, from my deep and
abiding childhood friends to the lonely years in Los Angeles to
my current state as a woman in her forties with a hard-fought
host of old friends, long distance friends, internet friends, and
new(ish) friends.

Long before there was a Life Council, there was just Laura,
a little girl in a tiny Oklahoma town with such deep anxiety
she pulled her hair out at the roots. A little girl whose most
important relationship was with her books.

And then, in the third grade, there was Lauren. My first
best friend.

I liked that her name was so similar to mine. I liked her
handwriting. I liked her big laugh and how she was good at creating choreography to popular songs that we would perform at
recess or in our respective living rooms. We had sleepovers and
sat together at lunch, and we wrote each other friendship love
notes with lots of bubble letters that got folded in complicated

and creative ways. I thought she was the smartest, prettiest, bestest best friend a nine-year-old girl could have. I still think that, even though we naturally drifted apart and had different interests and friend groups by the time we hit middle school.

Meeting Lauren when I was nine, along with the rest of my school friends, kicked off something fundamental in me. I'm an introvert who craves quiet, but the pull of being with friends remains irresistible. I love to be with people, love to laugh with them, love to hold eye contact in a deep conversation. I was initially a shy kid, but making friends slowly emboldened me. I became outgoing in the presence of my friends.

Starting with those formative childhood relationships, the friends I have made throughout my life have always played an outsized role. I grew up in a loving nuclear family, but my sister and brother are both nearly a decade older than I am, and we didn't have ties to our extended family. My parents worked, and with my siblings off at college before I hit double digits, my chosen friends have always been my primary source of connection. In every stage, it has been my friends I have looked to for guidance, fulfillment, and adventurous memories. Surrounding myself with strong friendships in which I am seen and known (and, likewise, getting to see and know others) is one of my greatest joys.

Friendship was served up to me on a silver platter when I was young. Between my hometown, church, summer camp, and college sorority, I rarely had to make a concerted effort to find friends. We were on the same team or in the same class or attending the same activity, so presence alone felt like inclusion. I assumed it would always be that way.

What I didn't understand about growing up in Oklahoma— and which I know now after living for more than twenty years in overpopulated Los Angeles—is that it's actually easier to make meaningful connections in smaller communities. I thought the opposite would be true. When I moved to Los Angeles after college, I was seeking more options in my relationships.

Adulthood was my friendship rude awakening. I wasn't automatically included in anything because there was no overarching organization I was a part of, nothing passively keeping anyone in touch or seeing one another regularly. Even my job in film and television production was freelance, so there was little time to bond with anyone as I jumped from project to project. I was learning that everyone was on their own after college, in every conceivable way. It was supposed to be friendship freedom, but it was really friendship famine.

I quickly learned that the girlfriend rules in Los Angeles for twenty-somethings were very different from those I'd mastered while making friends in Oklahoma. It was all about who you knew, who had what connections, and who could get your name on the list at the door of the hot new club. I moved to LA straight after college graduation and knew almost no one in the city other than my roommate, and it was harder to meet people than I imagined, let alone people who wouldn't judge my accent. Looking back, I was spending more time in bars (which I loathed) than bookstores (which I loved), so I'll take my share of the blame for looking for friends in all the wrong places. But Hollywood has a reputation for inauthenticity, and there's truth to that. My early years in California were littered with "friends" who had little depth and with whom I didn't stay in contact for more than a few months at a time. I missed the feeling of belonging I experienced in high school and college, so I set out to recreate it for myself in my new home.

During my first long-term television gig working for MTV, I tried to put together a group of similarly-aged, similar-ish people who worked in the building. I called it (literally) Let's Be Friends, and it was basically a series of happy hours. I thought it was a brilliant way to create a friendship group, and it was fun to host. We went dancing, we played bar trivia, we complained about our bosses. It had the makings of something fun, but it fizzled after just a few weeks. I couldn't tell you why—on paper, we were all a bunch of young LA transplants working long hours in the entertainment industry. But it never gelled, and I got tired of forcing it and begging people to come. I wonder now if I should have given it a little more time or if some things just aren't meant to be.

For a while, I leaned hard into my long-distance friends, maintaining daily email threads where we poured out hundreds of words a day. Those communications saved me. This was before texting and before social media, so it was fun to regale my friends back in Oklahoma with my daily stories of life in Hollywood. It served as both a journal and a touchstone. Without those emails where I turned my real life into some sort of long-form narrative, I'm not sure I would have stayed in California. Those old friends on the receiving end constantly encouraged me in my new life. Most of them were experiencing their own post-college growing pains, and touching base over email or a quick telephone call was enough to remind us of who we were: friends against the world. But at least we had each other.

After nearly three years in Los Angeles, I started to feel more like myself. I moved in with one of my dearest friends, Lindsay. She was my former college roommate, and she had moved to the West Coast the year after I did. Living with her again felt like home. Lindsay holds a special seat on my Life Council because there is a certain bond that forms between friends who live together for a long time, and an even stronger bond when you've both moved across the country to pursue your dreams. During the time we shared an apartment in Hollywood (which we could barely afford), we had a rotating cast of friends and boyfriends, and we threw epic parties that were far outside my comfort zone. We purposefully mashed up people we knew from work with acquaintances from the bar scene and neighbors down the block. It was a social time, and it was what I had imagined the single life in a big city would look like.

I also met some wonderful people (including my future husband) while working on the *jackass* movie franchise and subsequent television spinoff *wildboyz*, a job I secured within the first six months of arriving in LA. The *jackass* production cast and crew had been a team for years before I came on board, and they operated in a family-like atmosphere. It felt good to be a part of something creative and (believe it or not) meaningful. The shoot days were long, and I would definitely classify some of my friendships from that time as the Life Council category of Battle Buddies.

There came a shift, though, when I started dating the boss. I didn't report directly to Jeff Tremaine, but there was no doubt that he was in charge of *jackass: the movie*. We worked together for years before our relationship became romantic, but it undeniably changed my place on the familial crew. I was no longer anyone's friend; I was the boss's girlfriend. This stung, and I was bitter about it for a long time. I had poured years into those relationships that had, in some ways, come to define my time in Los Angeles. I hated to lose them because of my romantic choices, but once Jeff and I started dating, the damage was done between me and my fellow crew members, and I was devastated. I understand why the dynamic changed, but it felt unfair.

Eventually I left MTV and took a job on a popular nanny reality show for Fox. While working on that series, I had a group of Business Besties that made the project more enjoyable. We had lunch together every day and endured the chaos of making a network TV show, and for years, we saw each other more than we saw our own families or roommates. It was this group of friends that was with me to celebrate when Jeff proposed.

I went into my marriage with high hopes for the next stage of life. Jeff and I wanted to start a family quickly, we were renovating our 1920s home, and I was planning to make a run at being a writer, something that had eluded me since college. On the surface, we were living the LA dream. But inside, I became desperately lonely.

I had not anticipated the hole it would leave in my life when I resigned from the entertainment industry. All the friends I had made in the previous years were on set somewhere while I was at home, adjusting to marriage. Our free time no longer matched up, and we had less in common. Meanwhile, I struggled to get pregnant. The very reason I had left behind my job and friends wasn't materializing as I had planned.

It was an isolated, dark season, but ultimately, it changed my life. The two most important things I did to combat loneliness in those years were to start a book club and start a blog—both of which affected my entire trajectory. The blog led to full-time writing and eventually podcasting, and it introduced me to the friends who would have some of the greatest influence on my thirty-something decade and my career. The book club gave me in-person companionship paired with my passion for reading, as well as friends who pulled me out of my funk month by month at our marathon weekend meetings. I haven't stopped writing and talking about friendship since.

This isn't exactly a Happily Ever After, as I've had plenty of friendship ups and downs in the intervening years. Some of the hardest times of my life so far were those immediately following the births of my children, when postpartum struggles were all-consuming and kept me underwater. But the blog gave me an outlet to express those feelings and connect with other new moms, and the book club gave me something to look forward to on the calendar every month. These two things kept me afloat, and they were enough for a long time.

Until they weren't. Once my kids were a little older, and I was out of the mommy weeds of diapers and exhaustion, I started to cultivate friendships with a little more intention. It took a lot of trial and error. A lot of coffee dates and margarita meetups. I started to say yes when invited and started to issue my own invitations when I wasn't asked. And the effort slowly started to pay off. I began to see where I could be a better friend to others. I reached out more to long-distance friends and fostered more community with local friends.

By the time I turned forty, I had subconsciously assembled a type of Life Council. I messaged weekly with an old friend who had known me from childhood and met up regularly with a new friend who only knew the latest version of me. I had a friend who always let me tag along on her adventures and a friend who didn't mind spending hours verbally dissecting my latest obsession. Outside of my immediate family, my friendships were my most important relationships, and giving them so much priority fulfilled me in a way that marriage, motherhood, and my career couldn't. I was recognizing that my friendships were crucial to my overall happiness and well-being.

FRIENDSHIPS WERE CRUCIAL TO MY OVERALL HAPPINESS AND WELL-BEING.

I've learned enough to know that everything might change again the next time my life shifts. It all continues to be a journey. But even as the seats on my Life Council rotate or evolve, the system of surrounding myself with supportive women has grounded me in a way that will remain. This is more than just a concept. This is a foundation.

Five Friendship Philosophies

1. Friendship is a to-do
2. Believe the best
3. Just go
4. Like every selfie
5. Your spouse is not your best friend

We learned most of our friendship habits and ideas early in life, when caregivers plopped us on the floor and we were forced to get along with whatever sibling or playmate was on that blanket with us. We were most likely encouraged to share our toys, admonished not to hit one another, and told to stay in a general proximity. We weren't given much of a choice about when the playing began or ended, and all of this was the beginning of learning how to be in relationships with one another.

When we got to be school-age, friendship rules were explicitly spelled out and simple enough for everyone to understand.

We were taught to share, take turns, be inclusive, be kind. These are great rules for relationships. But if that was the last time anyone gave you clear instructions on how to be a good friend, there have surely been bumps in the road along the way since then.

As we grew, we probably went on to experience some sort of friendship angst in our younger years: friends moved away, friends hurt our feelings, we didn't get invited to the birthday, we were targeted by mean girls—or we were the mean girls ourselves. Or perhaps we didn't experience friendship drama so much as we didn't have any friends at all. Middle school can be rough.

In the teen years, the issues were more or less the same, but the stakes were higher. Our loneliness increased or our feelings were hurt more deeply. Hopefully we received well-meaning advice from our moms or sisters or teachers or summer camp counselors, but maybe not. We will carry what we learn about friendship in our earliest years into the rest of our lives. If we don't stay attuned to how things change, we will let old hurts and insecurities rule our emotions and actions in adulthood without making the allowance that everyone else has grown up, too. Every new and old friend you will ever have has a friendship past, just like you do, so it can be helpful to identify some general philosophies as guideposts for our friendships, especially for the seasons when we're struggling.

Time and circumstances require a little more nuance than the first friendship rules we learned in kindergarten.

I think it's a worthy experiment to think about your friendship philosophies from a grown-up perspective. Think about the rules you were taught about being a good friend, which are likely ingrained in you, and then ask yourself if you still believe them to be true. As you do this, you'll see that we're all operating from a set of friendship philosophies, whether we've formalized them or not. Start by brainstorming what you like about certain friendships, and then brainstorm what hasn't worked so well in the past. In the final section of the book, we're going to talk about what we value in individual people, but here we're talking about overall guidelines to help us bring our best selves to our relationships. In both of these exercises, you might surprise yourself by how you define what matters (and what doesn't).

My most important friendship philosophies are these:

Friendship Philosophy #1: Friendship Is a To-Do

This is a new practice for me, but it's one of the things I believe most helped my friendships over the last couple of years: Friendship is an item on your To Do list, just like cleaning the bathroom or getting your oil changed.

I do not want this to be true. I want to be a person who does friendship organically and wholeheartedly, a person who is generous and loving and known for her strong relational priorities. Alas, I'm actually an anxious, introverted working mother with a screen addiction and a tendency toward procrastination. The in-person, fun part of friendship comes naturally to me. The mundane work of it does not.

The truth is, friendship *is* work. People don't talk about

that enough. We hear about how marriage is work and parenthood is work, but somehow, maintaining healthy relations with our friends is supposed to be effortless, but I don't find that to be true. I *want* to remember that my friend is up for a promotion or that she's having a minor surgery next Tuesday or that her beloved cat just died, and I *want* to send flowers or a note or a text for all of these things, but without reminders, I will not. Maintaining care for the best friends in my life is emotional labor. Sometimes it's physical labor. It's not all margaritas and memories.

THE TRUTH IS, FRIENDSHIP *IS* WORK.

Oh yes, I've seen the memes that float around the internet about being (or wanting) a low-maintenance friend. And there are definitely seasons when you have to give all you can to your family or your job, and the work of friendship isn't something you can take on. I also see the value in having a decidedly low-maintenance friend with low expectations all around. But that's not going to go the distance. Someone is going to hit a rough patch. Someone is going to lose their job or get a divorce and need a shoulder and a hand. Someone is going to get a diagnosis. That someone might be you.

The work of friendship turns out to be worth it. When I started thinking about my closest friendships as part of my to-do list—not as a chore, but as a priority that needed to be attended to—my friendships changed. And my friends noticed.

I use a notepad for my daily To Do lists and on each page I have three sections: personal, work, and connection. The personal and work sections are self-explanatory, but the connection section usually has items listed like:

Text Yasmin
Vox Bri
Check Sarah's IG feed

Something like "Buy Ashley a birthday present" would be on my personal to-do list because that's a tangible to-do item and not really about connection in the same way.

I add people to the connection to-do list when they pop into my mind, or as a reminder to reach out for a specific reason. There's a circle of friends with whom I check in regularly (at least once a week), and then long-term or long-distance friends who hear from me once a month or so, and then a handful of people in my life whom I love dearly, but realistically, we only interact a few times a year. If they weren't on my to-do list, it might dwindle to even less than that.

In one of my recent friendship struggles, I had a good friend tell me candidly that being on my to-do list hurt her feelings. She wanted me to think of her instinctively, to reach out without prompting and not because I set an alarm in my calendar (something I'm also known to do). I was taken aback by her response because, if anything, I hope a friend would feel flattered that I am making an effort where I previously have so often dropped the ball, but she took it as a reduction of our spiritual bond.

I got defensive at first (of course), but then I sat with it and tried to understand where she was coming from. She wanted to feel like one of my best friends (which she is) and not simply someone on a list, which can feel like a drudgery. I wanted to stop feeling so flaky and had made some adjustments in my day and mindset in order to prioritize close relationships with people who do not live in my house. It was an impasse. We love one another dearly, but we think about life and relationships in very different ways. By the end of our thorny conversation, I believe we came to an understanding of each other's hearts in the matter, even if we still didn't completely grasp each other's point of view. She agreed to try to see my new tactics as an act of love and not a chore, and I agreed to make my check-ins with her seem less scheduled.

Your approach to the work of friendship might look different from mine, just like any item on your to-do list will look different from mine. But if we can give ourselves the tools to succeed in our most important relationships—including treating them by our actions with the same reverence with which we hold them emotionally—our friendships will be stronger and more deeply woven into the fabric of our lives.

Friendship Philosophy #2: Believe the Best

I believe all relationships go more smoothly when we assume positive intentions. I'm not trying to be unrealistically positive in the face of friendship complications, but when we jump to negative conclusions about a friend's behavior, we are often wrong and create a rift where there wasn't one. When something seems off with a friend—maybe they're not returning our texts or maybe they forgot our birthday or maybe we were on the receiving end of a casually snide remark—what if, instead of assuming that they're mad at us, that they no longer like us, that they're secretly out to get us, we assign neutral intent? It doesn't mean you're being naive or gullible if you decide that they're busy or that a comment wasn't personal.

We can actively choose to believe our friends have the best of intentions, just as we hope they would *believe the best* about us.

This doesn't mean we should always let these kinds of slights slide. By all means, we have every right to expect a friend to call us back and to not say hurtful things even if they're teasing. But unless it's a pattern in their behavior or character (which warrants a deeper look at continuing the friendship at all), believing the best in someone takes less energy than assuming the worst.

Trauma and past unhealthy situations may very well give us reason to be suspicious or defensive in our friendships. I'm sure we can all think of someone who has given us plenty of reason not to *believe the best* of them—or of anyone. I get it. But after my periods of not being the greatest friend myself, I'm grateful for those who gave me grace along the way. They knew I was simply overwhelmed when I had to cancel plans or exhausted when I spoke too sharply. Sometimes I was

> **BELIEVING THE BEST IN SOMEONE TAKES LESS ENERGY THAN ASSUMING THE WORST.**

called out; sometimes I realized the mistake and corrected it myself; sometimes my behavior was just ignored. But my close friends always came from a place of believing I was a good person with a good heart, and if they'd believed anything else, I'm not sure we could have overcome the offense.

My anxious brain defaults to assuming that someone is mad at me or that they're seconds away from being mad at me. When I was younger and much more judgmental of others, I thought everyone else was sitting in judgment too, and this made me do a constant tap dance of justification of my own actions and demand explanations for theirs. I used to keep score and wouldn't call, text, or email someone back if it was their turn. I didn't want to go to their birthday dinner if they'd blown off mine. I slowly grew out of the need for such strangling control over the people in my life, and that maturity was freedom. The next obvious step was to start continually believing in the best of intentions from those I wanted to assume good intentions from me.

Obviously, we don't want a friendship to be a one-way street, but sweating the small stuff in friendship is often a recipe for disappointment. I can't keep score with the people I love. It won't always be an even exchange. But in a healthy friendship, it all seems to shake out. If it doesn't? Well, that's worth further examination.

Sometimes our own insecurities cause us to be suspicious, territorial, and controlling. Deciding to *believe the best* in my friends and expecting them to *believe the best* in me has infused my relationships with love.

Friendship Philosophy #3: Just Go

This is a personal directive that has shifted over the years depending on my life circumstances, but I noticed decades ago that I rarely regret going to dinner or on the trip or to the party. And often, I do regret *not* going.

There are always reasons not to go: finances or a breast-feeding baby or a calendar conflict are legitimate excuses to bow out of anything. And sometimes we may need the self-care that comes with not going. But when we do go—even if it costs us some sleep or some money or is inconvenient—our very presence opens the door to connection and memory-making and being known as a person who shows up.

Because we cannot replace face-to-face time. Technology has given us a million ways to stay in touch and post photos and make video calls, which is better than not connecting at all. But *nothing* beats a hug, an in-person congratulations, or a shared conversation with every nuance of body language, laughter, and eye contact.

I put a high priority on the milestones in life, like weddings and funerals and other major events. I've decided that I must *just go* to those things, and unless there's a glaring reason to do so, I will not weigh the pros and cons or agonize over that decision. If it's within my ability to be there, I will. When I was growing up, this was a given. You go to people's big events. I'm not sure when it became optional. Maybe because events got more extravagant, therefore requiring more of the attendees' time, money, or effort, or because we've somehow decided that certain things don't matter anymore—but our presence *does* matter. There is a spiritual communion among friends when you show up for the big moments.

> THERE IS A SPIRITUAL COMMUNION AMONG FRIENDS WHEN YOU SHOW UP FOR THE BIG MOMENTS.

A few years ago, I made the effort to attend my high school reunion in Oklahoma, and I was shocked at who came and who didn't. People who were still local to our hometown didn't even attempt to swing by, while those of us who lived hundreds of miles away arrived with bells on. I know many people have no desire to attend reunions, but that weekend I reconnected with classmates I hadn't talked to in twenty years. Sure, we were Facebook friends. I already knew where they lived and how many kids they had, but the in-person energy could never be replicated through a screen. Stories came to the surface that never would have if we hadn't been sitting together, feeding off one another's collective memories. I flew back to California with a full heart and an even better understanding of my childhood.

I also have a group of far-flung friends I met on the internet—the same women who were there when Chris Ann taught us about Life Councils—who have played an enormous role in how I've approached friendship over the last ten years. Our troop started when we were all online blogging all day every day, and a decade later, our lives don't look like that anymore. It's been harder and harder to keep up as careers and kids keep us busier and busier, and some have abandoned social media altogether. But regardless of our internet habits, one thing we've maintained is an annual retreat weekend. We spend three days together with absolutely no agenda—just talking and eating and resting and laughing and catching up on all the things. I wait the whole year for that weekend to deeply connect with those women who mean so much to me. Sometimes I miss how it was in the beginning, when we all chatted through our screens every single day, but the yearly retreat goes a long way in keeping us close. The group is large enough that it's tough to nurture every individual relationship within it, so instead, I prioritize the in-person gathering. I'm committed to attending that weekend every year that I'm able because this is part of my *just go* philosophy.

The big stuff is a given: *Just go.*

What about the smaller stuff? Grabbing coffee, a last-minute double date, a dinner or a walk or a football game watch party? Sometimes I think we wait for the "perfect" opportunity to be joyfully spontaneous, but that's just not going to happen. When a casual plan starts to come together, you may not love the choice of restaurant or everyone else who is invited or the last-minute timing. You have to decide for yourself if it works for you, but don't overthink it. Ask yourself if you'll regret not going, and be honest about how much your attendance or absence will affect your relationships.

I'm not suggesting you sacrifice your schedule, sleep, and bank account for every little thing, but attendance is part of cultivating relationships. We cannot complain about our loneliness when we're picky about when we'll bless others with our presence. It's also true that the consistency of being together builds deeper friendships, much more so than infrequent meetups.

Just go! Err on the side of relationship.

Friendship Philosophy #4: Like Every Selfie

This phrase is taken from the poem by David Gate that opens this book, and while the whole piece has become a guiding beacon for me in the last two years with my friendships, these lines in particular make up the core of this philosophy:

Like every selfie
All of them
Clap their songs
Cheer them on
You were born with a limitless
Supply of encouragements
Use every one of them

When I first read this poem on Instagram, not only did it touch my soul, it also gave me an immediate directive. *Like every selfie. All of them.*

Look, I understand that cheering on our friends isn't always as simple as that. Sometimes we have resentments or jealousies or secondhand embarrassment about the way friends act (or post online). Sometimes we don't want to encourage them in the wrong direction if it seems like the new career or romance or hairstyle isn't in their best interest. It can be exhausting to fulfill an obligation to "like every selfie." It can feel inauthentic when you don't *really* like whatever it is they're putting out.

But does it matter? Are we culture critics who need to reserve our five-star reviews? Our honest and thoughtful reputations are not in danger when we tell a friend they look fabulous regardless of our actual opinion. There's a time and place for intervention—like when we become truly concerned about a friend's decisions—but most of our daily lives include hundreds of little ways to encourage someone. "Likes" and high fives and quick text emojis are a low bar for all of us to feel generous and for others to feel like we care (because we do). Not to mention that withholding such generosity can feel like poison.

In one of my informal Instagram polls, my messages exploded when I posed the question, "Do you notice when friends don't like, comment, or react to your posts?" The responses were all over the place—a fair mix between not caring at all and lengthy stories of how hurtful it feels when friends and family (who are otherwise active online) refuse to react to what we share on social media. In all of the various conversations I host on the internet, this one had the widest range of shame and vitriol spilling from the comments. It was fascinating to read all the rules and walls and justifications we've constructed around online behavior.

Since we can all agree that social media interactions cannot replace in-person relationships, and also that within years, these trends and platforms will be completely obsolete, you'd think none of it should carry much weight in our friendships. And yet here I am, making it one of my five friendship philosophies.

Of course, it's not really about the "likes" or the selfies. It's about the big and small ways we can cheer on one another without getting into an emotional tangle about it. It's a reminder to myself that not everything has to be so overanalyzed and that, in fact, this analysis is killing our instinctive connections.

IT'S ABOUT THE BIG AND SMALL WAYS WE CAN CHEER ON ONE ANOTHER.

So now, I do not waste one second of my life with my finger hovering over the like button (metaphorically or literally) when it comes to my friends. If there's a chance to cheer them on, I take it.

Friendship Philosophy #5: Your Spouse Is Not Your Best Friend

I developed this philosophy after expecting Jeff to be my everything early on in our marriage led to some intense loneliness. I remind myself of this tenet whenever I've gone too long without catching up with a friend or going out for a girls' dinner or when some sappy social media post has me in my feelings about the way other couples exist in their marriages.

Whenever I share that my spouse is not my best friend, I

get either a chorus of *amens* or people who secretly think my marriage is in trouble. In the end, this may just be a difference in marriage dynamics and labels, but I like to talk about this topic as a way to release the cultural idea that your life partner *should* be your best friend. There's nothing wrong if your marriage has an entirely separate energy than your friendships. My husband, Jeff, is not my best friend, and our marriage got better once I identified that.

Now, when someone declares they've "married their best friend," I inwardly cringe. We all know what they mean. They married the person they feel closest to in the world. Maybe it even has a double meaning, in that they were friends before they were lovers. That's my love story with Jeff: we were close friends for two years before anything romantic transpired between us.

And yet, Jeff is still not my best friend. We've been married for fifteen years, and he is the most important person in my life. He's my first call with good or bad news. He's my most trusted sounding board. He's my partner. But he is not my best friend. Maybe this is all semantics. Maybe it hinges on how one defines a "best friend" (and whether they find it romantic to marry one's best friend). I feel strongly on this issue because, in the first years of our marriage, I fell into the trap of wanting Jeff to be my "best" friend (after all, our relationship was built on those previous years of friendship), but I quickly found out that expecting one person to fulfill all of the most important roles of adult relationships left us both frustrated. It was unfair for him and lonely for me.

The best friends I've had throughout my lifetime—at any age—fill my cup in a way my husband does not. I am a distinctive version of myself with my friends, and our conversations together are wildly different from those with any romantic partner. Jeff doesn't understand four-hour dinners that include crying and belly laughing and long stories with too many tangents. He doesn't want to engage in the hours of analysis my friends and I spend covering the minutiae of our childhoods or whether we should cut bangs. (One of the great benefits of my best friends is that our discussions can vacillate between our traumas and our current style choices with ease.) For what it's worth, I'm not interested in most of the conversations he has or activities he engages in with his best friends, either.

This also isn't completely gender-specific. My oldest friend, Drew, was a groomsman in my wedding. We grew up in the same small town. Drew is now a scientist in New York City. He's been the other half of my marathon gab sessions since he started to walk me home in the third grade, and we have a verbal shorthand that moves too quickly for Jeff to catch. He is one of my best friends, and he is not my husband.

So maybe the difference here is about romantic friendships versus platonic ones. With my husband, there's a constant underlying attraction that becomes sexual chemistry, and then there are also the day-to-day, mundane parts of our life that include co-parenting, household duties, and crafting a future together. It's a partnership that has different complexities than a friendship.

Friendships have their own sets of obligations, but those usually don't demand major decision-making together. My friends and I may try to keep things fair by splitting the check or divvying up the task list for a trip or party, but we're not looking at the big picture of money or family or lifetime dynamics. Time with friends mostly nets fun, while time with my spouse is so ongoing that it just *is*.

Our marriage worked a lot better when I realized I needed to have best friends outside of my marriage. I needed to talk and laugh and connect and spend time with people who didn't share a bathroom with me. I appreciated my marriage more when I had other important people in my life who knew me on a soul level.

Jeff and I fought less when he wasn't my whole world. The pressure I put on both of us during my lonely years could have sunk us both. And believe me, Jeff is relieved I have people who will chatter on with me for hours. I feel lucky that I can do the chattering and then return home to crawl into bed with the person I've created a life with.

I APPRECIATED MY MARRIAGE MORE WHEN I HAD OTHER IMPORTANT PEOPLE IN MY LIFE WHO KNEW ME ON A SOUL LEVEL.

These two things work in harmony in more ways than one. Jeff is quick to notice if a friendship brings me joy and peace or if it's draining. My friends aren't afraid to ask what's going on in my marriage. There is a checks and balances among these relationships that can be useful for seeing what is hard to see for yourself.

Years ago, upon returning home from yet another girls' weekend where I was weepy and annoyed, Jeff gently suggested that maybe I stop going on that annual adventure. It had been awhile since I'd enjoyed it, but I wasn't willing to admit that maybe these particular women and I were growing apart. I probably would have gone on that same girls' trip every spring until the end of time and never considered that stepping away was an option, especially since Just Go! is one of my most important friendship philosophies. It took someone who saw me every day to see that the trip was defeating and not uplifting.

Likewise, after a rough patch in our marriage, I sat on the counter in my kitchen and told three of my Life Council friends that marriage was hard, and I was done putting any effort into it. I didn't want a divorce, but I was done trying to make it better all the time. Whatever happened, happened. They listened thoughtfully and then reminded me that I was really, really tired. That winter, I was exhausted. There was a lot going on in our lives, and it felt easier to blame it on Jeff than to work on some of the hard things. My friends didn't try to convince me that my marriage venting was wrong, but in some ways, they could see the situation more clearly than I could.

My best friends grant me laughter and grace that isn't tangled up in who made the vet appointment or how messy the bedroom is, and the affirmation of those friendships allows me to function with less neediness in my marriage. This is a core friendship philosophy for me because it's a reminder that we need more than one close relationship in our lives. When I'm out of sorts with family life, I plan a dinner with my friends to spend a few hours just being *me*.

My spouse is my spouse, and my best friends are my best friends. They're not the same thing, and all of my relationships are better for it.

•   •   •

These are the philosophies that are most important to my friendships, and once I'd clarified them, it made many relationship decisions easier. Note that some philosophies may change over time or when you move into a new season of life. How we behave online in our friendships is a part of the conversation that didn't exist twenty years ago but is a regular part of navigating relationships now. The etiquette surrounding this changes regularly—enough to make some people give up on the "social" part of social media entirely—but in my own life, it's something I want to pay attention to. I also had different friendship philosophies when I was single in my twenties and when I was drowning in my thirties than I have now in my forties. Sometimes it takes a little time to realize that your priorities or your own behaviors have changed.

For example, as a young adult, I cared a lot about trustworthiness. In my post-college years, as I was "finding myself," I held a lot of secrets and discretion was a must. With more life experience, the secure knowledge that everyone has their own "stuff," and nearly two decades of sharing myself on the internet, my ideas of privacy have definitely morphed. Of course, I still need to be able to trust my friends, but in my forties, this is more about their character than nitpicking individual actions. I am no longer suspicious of people's trustworthiness because I rarely make friends at this stage who don't have a trustworthy nature.

Also, the types of friendship we're drawn to naturally shifts with life stages. During the baby and toddler years, I desperately wanted new friends, but the effort it took to get to know someone was beyond my reach during those seasons of sleepless nights. I leaned heavily on people who already knew me and whom I already knew. I wish someone had given me permission to let that be enough back then because now that my kids are older, I have more space in my life for new friendships.

Brainstorm some of your own friendship philosophies, guideposts, or principles. Think about behaviors and rules you're already abiding by (such as always picking up when friends call or taking them out for a birthday lunch each year), and go from there. Being honest with yourself about personality and capacity will be more effective than trying to force yourself to fit into the box that movies and culture tell us friendship looks like. You may decide that some of your friendship habits are ready for a refresh.

Committing friendship philosophies to paper is by no means a requirement to strengthening your own relationships, but it was a helpful exercise for me. If you just have no idea where to start, pay attention to your friendships over the next few weeks or months, and notice what works well and what could use some improvement.

Now that you've learned about my friendship history, my recent friendship foibles, and the philosophies I've built for approaching my friendships, let's look at the ten types of friendships I am prioritizing, the people I've christened my Life Council.

PART II

The Life Council

What Is the Life Council?

The Life Council is a selection of friends who fulfill various roles in your life. They are the friends you can call upon when needed. Similar to a Board of Directors of a company or institution, your Life Council offers guidance and a variety of expertise that provides perspective and companionship on an otherwise lonely journey. The knowledge these friends offer can cover everything from the practical to the spiritual. Your relationship with each member of your council fills your life with meaning and love.

The Life Council is an idea. There is no literal call to order in a meeting of ten friends, at least not in my life. Although there have certainly been times when I could have benefitted from an in-person gathering of these ten trusted advisors, the Life Council I've laid out is simply a concept to help you think about your friendships in an organized way that fills you with permission and gratitude.

We know that the most effective councils have members with different roles, visions, and assets. So what if we looked at our friends and let their best qualities shine in our relationships? Instead of wishing our most sensible friend was more fun or our most fun friend was more sensible, what if we firmly decided that their best qualities are exactly what we need on our Life Council? We don't need one friend to hold all ten seats. We can't expect ourselves to occupy all ten seats for anyone else.

The ten archetypes I've created here come from my own experience and desires, and the friends I describe are real people. They're meant to simply be a starting place for you to figure out the seats on your own Life Council. The goal is not to fit our friends into some sort of stereotypical box, but rather to see their strengths and focus on the joy they bring to our lives. The point of identifying one person as a Yes Friend and one person as a Daily Duty Friend isn't to shrink their influence but to allow the friendship to thrive as one main thing. Every friend and friendship can serve a unique purpose and fulfill us in a singular way. An Old Friend and a Mentor have different roles to play, and while there may occasionally be some crossover, there doesn't have to be. As you're reading, I hope you have a lightbulb moment or two about why a certain friendship is so special. I hope you also start to understand what strengths and joy *you* might be bringing to your friends' Life Councils.

It sounds so simple. Perhaps you're sure you do this already. But do you? In the conversations I host online, I hear a lot of angst about friend expectations and disappointments when we don't exactly align with how to act and how to care. Our standards are often very high. Looking at our friendships as a whole—as a Life Council—might help.

When I first started telling people about the concept for this book, more than once I was met with dismay over the idea of having ten friends to fill different roles. One person actually gasped. *Ten friends?* they said. *I don't even have three good friends, let alone ten!* Before they heard one more word about it, they were already consumed with the scarcity of their friendships.

I want to emphasize that you do not need to have all the seats on your Life Council filled at the same time. Some of them—like the Mentor or the Fellow Obsessive—even lend themselves to being temporary. Do not start by deciding none of this applies to you. The Life Council idea can meet all of us where we are, in friendship abundance or in times of loneliness.

We do not need to give our friends titles. Sometimes we carry a lot of baggage with declaring anyone a "best" anything. Maybe phrases like "Battle Buddy" and "Business Bestie" seem juvenile to you. Don't get all tangled up in this. Brainstorming the members of your Life Council is meant to be fun.

The one thing I really want you to do while reading is to think of the many people who have made a difference in your life. Whether or not you would classify them as a friend or coworker or simply someone you used to know, part of assembling your Life Council is taking stock of those who have influenced you and realizing how those relationships have shaped your life. The next step is to think about the roles that aren't quite filled but which you crave. Don't have a Yes Friend? Keep your eyes open for one. Out of touch with an Old Friend? This book will inspire you to reach out. If you have a dear friend who holds a worthy title on your Life Council, but she doesn't quite fit any of my descriptions here, let there be a moment when you tell her exactly what you love about her.

By the time you're done reading through all ten Life Council members, I hope you feel gratitude for those already in their roles and motivated to fill any empty seats. Friendship is a cornerstone of our health and happiness. So let's make it a priority. Let's seat a Life Council.

The Daily Duty Friend

The Daily Duty Friend might be the most recognizable character on the council, but I was nearly forty years old—and a decade into parenthood—before I had the type of Daily Duty Friend I'd always envisioned.

As the name implies, a Daily Duty Friend is someone who is a part of your regular, everyday life. Not a long-distance friend, not a special-occasion, girls-night-every-other-month friend. She's a friend who doesn't blink to see you without a bra in midafternoon or who doesn't pause in speaking as she tiptoes around the toys and laundry that litter the family room floor. She's the friend who has memorized the days you get off work early or who grabs an extra bottle of your favorite shampoo when it's on sale. (And then leaves it randomly on your kitchen counter without explanation.) This is how pop culture depicts adult women friendships all the time, but the Daily Duty Friend is a pretty special relationship. If you happen to read this description and think, "This sounds like most of my friends," then consider yourself lucky.

Here's the thing about the Daily Duty Friend, though: her superpower is her daily-ness. She doesn't have to necessarily fit into any other category. She doesn't have to be a Soul Sister to reach the level of comfort that knows where your dust bunnies accumulate. She just has to be present regularly. The very proximity is what makes the friendship intimate.

Of course, your Daily Duty Friend might look very different from mine because our life circumstances are unique. Your Daily Duty Friend might be your upstairs neighbor whose mood you are able to judge just by the sound of her footsteps across your living room ceiling. Your Daily Duty Friend might be a crossover with your Business Bestie because you both spend so much time working. Your Daily Duty Friend might be someone from your carpool or who is on the same volunteer committee or is a fellow sports parent who always saves you a spot in the bleachers. Your Daily Duty Friend might not be someone you would otherwise choose, but they're in your life daily for whatever reason, so reframing the idea that this is a good thing could be a nice exercise.

Daily Duty Friends carry a lot of weight in our overall relationship structures, but it doesn't seem like such a heavy lift because it's amortized over the daily-ness of it all. The Daily Duty Friends—since, if you have one, you probably also are one—are the ones who carry us through the weeks, months, and years that make a life.

Most of us understand the Daily Duty Friend long before we recognize their value because some of our earliest friendships are daily duty by nature. When we first start to choose real friends, we're usually school-age, so we see that person for eight hours a day every weekday. It's a crash course in friendship, and it's awesome. Lunchtime and recess and the overall shared experience of having the same teacher and learning the same stuff under the umbrella of the same institution gives us a lot in common every single day, five days a week. It seems like all friendships should be this way—forever! Let's trade juice boxes and fruit snacks until the end of time.

Even as we get older and activities, interests, and studies diverge, for as long as we're in school—for roughly the first two decades of our lives—daily friendship comes easily because there's something outside of ourselves that dictates our time together. It's only after our school years are over that we notice daily, casual friends aren't just around without some effort. Even if you have roommates as a young adult, the friendship pool shrinks vastly overnight without a school connection. I think this is why that time period can be the beginning of our struggles with the intentionality of adult friendship.

My first daily friends came along in elementary school, and, since I'm from a small town, they stayed daily acquaintances until we graduated from high school. These people knew my parents and where we kept the spare house key and my score on the last math test. Some of them were true friends in the traditional sense of the word, but others were just people we knew. Everybody knew everybody, and I would have no more dreamed of classifying any of those people in Life Council categories than I would force myself to eat gravel. They were just daily people. By the time I left home, I was seriously sick of everybody knowing my middle name and remembering that year I permed my hair and got glasses at the same time, but I now see that type of knowing one another as the gift that it was. The daily-ness of small-town life is something I still ache for.

In my young adulthood, I had a series of roommates, both

in college and during my early years in Los Angeles. There is no one more Daily Duty than roommates, whether you like one another or not. You grow attuned to each other's grooming habits and sleep schedule and, well, you know, all the stuff that comes with living with someone. In the best of times, you share the cleaning and binge-watch stuff together. In the worst of times, all the daily-ness can feel like you're never alone, and perhaps you would choose loneliness over one more cold shower after someone else used all the hot water.

But after I got married, and the novelty of having the ultimate roommate who knows all the things about me inside and out wore off, I entered the loneliest phase of my life. I couldn't have articulated then that what I was missing was a Daily Duty Friend. I probably would have told you that I was craving a Soul Sister, a Business Bestie, or, hell, even a Yes Friend. And believe me, I would have welcomed any of those to accompany my quiet days while my new husband was away working for weeks at a stretch. What I really needed was a regular companion. Someone to volley a thought to. Someone to toss another one back. I was twenty-eight years old, my life stretched out in front of me, and deep in my soul, I believed I'd chosen a lonely life in Los Angeles over a connected life in Oklahoma.

I believed that for a long, long time.

I'm not sure I would have believed that Daily Duty Friends existed anymore if I didn't see with my own eyes that people I knew had them. I was in a book club with two longtime best friends from college who called each other multiple times a day and did errands together on the weekends and had impromptu dinners and trips and such. I loved being in a book club with them, but their bond was impossible to breach.

They were each other's Daily Duty Friends. Three would have been a crowd.

When we bought a lake house in South Carolina the year after we were married, I jumped into the deep end of Daily Duty Friends. Our tiny little lake town was full of friendly faces, many of whom entered our life with regular invitations to grill and tube and grab dinner and sit on the porch while the sun set. I immediately loved those people and their obvious care for one another and how they opened their circle so wide for us. But we were just the summer folk. We got to play at being a part of their daily lives for a few months each year. Their real duty was to one another, all year long, and it was unwavering.

Even after I had one baby, and then two, and secretly harbored a hope that mommydom would bring the Daily Duty Friends calling, I found that it wasn't the culture in the particular circle of parenthood I found myself in. I did the Mommy and Me classes, and the meet-at-the-park playdates, but women are fiercely protective of their kids and their time in Los Angeles. In spite of the politics of the West Coast, I did not find a village of the kind I had observed in the parts of the country where people vote like it doesn't take one. It was a strange dichotomy of philosophy, where we didn't share snacks or swap birthing horror stories. There was a competitiveness I hadn't expected among mothers in LA. Your organic baby blanket was yours and yours alone.

By the time my kids were out of diapers, I had given up hope on mimicking the female friendship model from my youth. I wasn't really lonely anymore—I had pulled myself out of that hole slowly, one month and one blog post at a time. I was blogging and running a book club and pouring into my childhood friends, even across five states. Somewhere along the way, I'd decided that the friends I had were enough—they were long distance or mostly on a screen, but they really filled me up. I had some local friends, too, not the deepest of relationships but women to grab drinks with, and the moms who were at all the same toddler birthday parties. I had found a rhythm and liked it. I didn't even think about loneliness anymore. I felt pretty mature that I'd made the most of my relationships, even if they weren't what I had pictured. And then came Julie.

Julie was part of a wider group of mom friends I made when my daughter, Lucy, started at a new elementary school. We got to know one another gradually, through school activities and moms' nights out. Our girls were still young enough to require fairly supervised playdates, so we'd spend a few hours at a time at my house and a few hours at hers, pulling out cheese and chocolate from Trader Joe's, and the time always flew by. Julie and I had a surprising amount in common, given that she was a second-generation Vietnamese-American and raised in Los Angeles, so different from my own upbringing. We had similar style—though hers was a bit more sophisticated—down to owning the exact same eclectic pieces in our closets, which we purchased years before meeting. We had similar taste in men—our husbands, as it turned out, were alike in some very specific ways, so we instinctively understood each other's marriage dynamics. And we had given our daughters the same name. We both had little Lucys, and they, too, at least on the inside, were very similar.

Now, if you spent a few minutes with me and Julie, especially before we became Daily Duty Friends, you might not agree that we're very much alike. Julie is gentle and careful with her words. She exudes kindness, has a bright, open face, understated hair and makeup, and she is quietly magnetic. I can count half a dozen women who believe Julie is their best, most Daily Duty Friend. I, on the other hand, often forget to think before I speak, frequently balance my messy, unbrushed hair with startlingly bright lipstick, and have been told my vibe is "unapproachable."

But Julie and I think a lot alike. We often come to the same conclusions about people and the news headlines and elementary-level sports. Our eyes meet, and we just *know* what the other is thinking. We were just getting to know each other when she broke the news that their family had decided to move to Amsterdam. As happy as I was for their new adventure, inside I was crushed. Julie and I were becoming really close, and the move didn't bode well for a long-term friendship. I knew we would keep in touch—and we downloaded all the apps to make it so—but I also knew what can happen to new friendships that are kept out of sight for too long. They're regulated to another category altogether: long-distance acquaintances.

In the year after Julie's family moved to Amsterdam, we kept up loosely online, but as predicted, the time zones and radically different daily life experiences made it hard to maintain the same amount of closeness we had been building. We traveled to Amsterdam to visit their family the next summer, and when they told us they were returning to Los Angeles, I let out a breath I didn't know I was holding.

Julie's family had been back in California just eight months when the pandemic struck. When Los Angeles went into strict lockdown, all of our Daily Duty friendships suffered. Our group of mom friends—all with kids in the fourth grade at that point—tried to keep up with FaceTime happy hours and regular text chain check-ins, but of course it was hard.

We got together for the occasional backyard drink or socially distanced walk, but there was a lot of fear in the air, and our days suddenly looked different than ever before, as we were managing multiple kids schooling from home among other things.

In the fall of 2020, Julie's husband found a club volleyball program that was proceeding while most other team sports had temporarily shut down. We all agreed that our girls could use the stimulation and movement, so Jeff and I let our Lucy try out, even though our family knew absolutely nothing about the sport. When both Lucys made the volleyball team, Julie and I entered a whole new world of Daily Duty friendship.

Jeff and I had always sworn we wouldn't do club sports. It's a ton of commitment, non-exciting travel, and requires an intensity we don't always possess. And yet there we were, jumping in with both feet. In our defense, we might have stuck to our original guns if not for the pandemic. I think our whole family was looking for something that felt fun and normal.

Both of the Lucys thrived learning volleyball, and soon our two families had a carpool schedule and a text thread navigating the complicated world of club tournaments. We took turns driving the girls, feeding the girls, letting the girls sleep over; it was a quick entanglement of both families, and I loved the familiarity.

Eventually, Lucy and Lucy returned to school when it opened, and we all had new layers of things to juggle as the world slowly opened back up. Julie and I texted or talked every day about the logistics of who was driving when, should I feed your child or no, can you also grab this or that if you're out and I'll pay you back, and how do you feel about what we overheard the kids discussing last week?

I hadn't had a Daily Duty Friend since Lindsay (see: The Soul Sister) and I lived together in our twenties. I'd certainly never had a Daily Duty Friend in parenthood who was also helpful and in the trenches with me (see: The Battle Buddy). Beyond volleyball, meals, and travel, Julie and I also had another kid each, were parents at the same school, and were part of the same larger friend group. There was always something to discuss. It had been so long since I had a friend who really understood what my daily life looked like. It made me feel less alone in the boring tasks of day-to-day life because someone else was keeping up and interested.

I love that Julie has memorized the gate code to my house and my kids' In-N-Out order. I love that we can talk about our dogs at length. It is always funny to me when we show up wearing the same exact outfit, and if, for some reason, we haven't talked for a few days, we call and exclaim that it's been *so long*.

As I write this, Julie and I are on the precipice of our Daily Duty friendship changing shape. Lucy and Lucy have chosen different middle schools to attend, and their volleyball futures are also in flux. We have acknowledged to one another that we're potentially at the end of an era and have both already started to grieve that. We're not worried about staying friends—our bond is too deep for that, so I know we will. But the daily-ness of it all was too brief.

• • •

Long before I met Julie, our family had a Daily Duty Friend who put in the work, year after year, and taught me what it means to be a chosen family. Jeff has known Rick since the '90s, when they worked at a skateboard magazine together.

Rick went on to work with Jeff as a photographer and cameraman and featured talent in a number of movies and TV shows, including the *jackass* franchise. They've been buddies for thirty years.

When Jeff and I got married and started a family, it was an anomaly to most of his local friend group. Like a lot of them, Rick was single and without kids, and I think Jeff settling down into family life felt to some like he was bowing out of the late-night camaraderie of the bachelors. There was that natural drift that occurs when friends' lives change.

But Rick's devotion to Jeff and his new family never wavered. He was there in the days after we brought Lucy home from the hospital and then again when we brought home Finch, bearing hand sanitizer and a stuffed animal. From the time they were swaddled infants to this exact moment, Rick has made an enormous effort in his *de facto* uncle status. He shows up nearly every weekend we're in town just to say hi and see the kids. He brought his guitar when they were babies and would stay if I needed to run an errand or just take a nap. He remembers their birthdays and plans their Christmas gifts months in advance.

This is a different sort of Daily Duty Friend. It's less about the minutiae of our lives and more about choosing to be a part of someone's family when, frankly, it would be easier not to. Jeff and I have stayed in awe of Rick's commitment to our family over the years, when the obvious choice for a single guy would be less involvement. But none of us have blood relations in Los Angeles, and choosing to stay so intimately involved in one another's lives has filled a void for all of us, I think. Rick's love for us is an action. It's steady and, I really must emphasize, it's completely chosen.

I think about that as we begin the next stage in our family's life at a new school in a new neighborhood, and I wonder what it would look like if I didn't let circumstances dictate my Daily Duty Friends, but instead created them. If I tried to talk to someone every day by choice and not necessity, and if, over time, it would mean our lives were interwoven from the frequent contact and care, like Rick is woven into the fabric of our family.

Once you've had a Daily Duty Friend, it's hard to imagine life without one. Being in such a close relationship with Julie for the last couple of years has given me so much life—it has filled my cup and reminded me of the fun of the daily friendships I had when I was young. This seat on the Life Council might be filled for you already, or maybe it's gotten your wheels turning on what this type of friendship would mean to your long days. Either way, I hope for us both a lifetime of friendships that are more than just occasional, because who we are in our every day is who we are in our lives.

The Old Friend

They make movies about old friends. They write songs about old friends. Whole books are dedicated to the analysis of famous friendships in history. Old friends are considered the gold standard of relationships merely because they've lasted through the decades, and I get it. Longtime friends have been witness to multiple iterations of ourselves, and that knowledge—the before and the after, the total trajectory—is priceless. It can't be bought or replaced. That's why old friends get to wear the bridesmaid dresses, get to be in the room when no one else is, and stay on the short list of people to be notified on the occasion of big events, even if you're not quite in touch like you used to be.

I understand the value of old friends, to have one and to be one. I also understand that because they're not a Life Council member one can create—by nature, they must already exist—this chair might not always be filled for everyone in the same way.

Statistically, most of us probably have old friends. That is to say, there are humans we have known for many years. But they might not be people you want on your Life Council.

And considering different ages and lifestyles, one person's Old Friend might be another's (relatively) New Friend. There's not a hard-and-fast rule determining what makes a friend "old" or not, but in this case, I'm defining it primarily as **someone who has seen you through at least one stage into another.** From style evolutions such as bad haircuts and suspect fashion choices to the more painful transitions between schools, jobs, romances, belief systems, and neighborhoods, old friends "knew us when" and are still around to talk about it.

Reading stories about old friendships may highlight a lack of them in your life or may remind you of someone who was once there and now is not. For those who feel this will always be a hole on your Life Council, keep in mind two things: (1) "old" is subjective, and it's possible to consider someone who has been in your life for the last few years to be your Old Friend, and (2) use this pain point as an opportunity to start investing in friendships that you think will go some distance. In what feels like the blink of an eye, those people will become your Old Friends.

I'm lucky enough to have lots of spots on my Life Council for old friends. Growing up in a small town makes it nearly impossible to become unacquainted with people you knew when you were a child, but I've done more than just stay in touch with these friends of my youth. I've maintained a real reverence for these friendships, partly because my old friends are incredible people, but also because they keep me in touch with my core self. I've gone through phases of trying on different sides of my identity, and living in Hollywood can really wreck your sense of self, so it's my old friends who keep me the most grounded. I simply cannot be anyone but who I am in their presence. As a natural wanderer, it's a blessing to have so many tethers.

When we were twelve years old, people thought Kimi and I were twins. Well, we might have embellished that history a bit, but for sure people thought we were related. We definitely looked enough alike to pass as relatives, with our long, skinny limbs, round faces, and straight hair. We dressed alike, too, both trying (and failing) to hide our lack of curves under loose-fitting, baggy styles. Kimi and I even carried ourselves similarly, sort of nerdy meets self-confident meets silly-is-the-new-cool. It was really no wonder that fellow campers and counselors started to associate us together at the summer camp where we met.

It just took one interaction to notice our glaring difference back then: Kimi was the city girl to my country mouse. We might be spending months together in the Ozarks singing "Kumbaya," but Kimi was wearing J.Crew and I was wearing Walmart, and although she never made mention of it, I was certainly aware. I suffered from a lot of childhood anxiety, and my fears always flared at camp, making me skittish and hypersensitive. As Kimi remembers it, she was still reeling from her parents' divorce, and those were scars that hadn't yet healed. It was a sensitive time for both of us, maybe. But since it blossomed in the bubble of a summer camp world, the things that might have made our friendship more complicated in the real world ceased to matter. We were alike in so many ways and enjoyed being regarded as sisters, so we role-played the "twins" thing up. Camp also provided the cover for us to be simply ourselves without the daily pressures of teenager-ness and home life. Twelve people living in an open cabin leaves little room for pretense.

The months we spent together at camp are some of my greatest childhood memories. Over the years we laughed, we danced, we canoed, we sang, and then we laughed some more. We shared every meal, and every activity felt like a bonding experiment. For a long time, summer camp was a little sanctuary, and Kimi and I remained campers long past the average age. As we neared high school graduation, we made conscious plans for the future of our friendship.

We wanted to go to college together at either Baylor or the University of Oklahoma, but at the last minute, we both panicked. She ended up at Baylor, and I ended up at the University of Oklahoma, which was the right decision for both of us. In the summers between college semesters, we worked together at the camp where we'd met and turned our twin-ness into something more official, launching a comedy act for the campers called Polly Popular and Carla Copier. We dressed up in ridiculous matching outfits, and Kimi (as Carla) chased me (as Polly) around the stage in skits about being your own individual person. The messaging was clear to the kids, but I think we just enjoyed dressing alike on purpose for a crowd.

As Kimi and I got older, our friendship transcended our summer camp life. While other relationships from that same season couldn't quite make the leap from canoe trips to cubicles and kids, Kimi and I never missed a beat. In some ways, the fact that our friendship began in a vacuum helped us see one another more clearly. Our friendship wasn't shaped by our home lives, our families, or our school friends. We had come to know one another deeply just as we were. It's a rare bond I don't have with anyone else.

After college, Kimi married a boy we worked with at camp. The wedding was full of old friends from our summer days—and all the drama, entanglements, and dumb behavior that comes when people who know each other in one environment are suddenly thrown into an entirely different one and told to thrive. We survived that weekend together, and a few short years later, she wore pink tulle to walk down the aisle at *my* wedding, where her very presence brought me peace amidst the celebration chaos, the way only old friends can do.

As time has marched on, Kimi and I look less alike in pictures but have remained remarkably in sync in every fundamental way. We became mothers the same year. We visited one another's homes and found that we had decorated with some of the same unusual pieces. We endured heartbreaking losses and challenging family dynamics and once went a long stretch without talking for no reason other than we were both busy, and when we did catch up, it turned out we had changed religious and political beliefs in the same way without ever discussing it.

There's no pressure for Kimi and I to stay on similar paths—we've always been happy to let the other person be whoever she is. It just keeps happening naturally because the spirit that attracted us to one another when we were twelve still lives on in each of us as forty-somethings. I suspect it will for the rest of our lives.

Kimi is now a successful business owner with three kids in Dallas, and we don't get to see one another much anymore—once every few years if we're lucky. Before one of us calls the other on the phone, we text ahead of time to assure that it's not an emergency so as not to scare one another with out-of-the-blue phone calls. And yet, when there is an emergency, I will call Kimi. Or someone will call her for me. She is on my shortest list of People Who Need to Know because, as one of my oldest friends, she has known the most versions of me. Even if I didn't feel as spiritually connected to her as I do, this catalog of information is enough to earn her a seat on my Life Council.

●　●　●

The Old Friend seat on my Life Council is co-chaired, so to speak. Most of these friendships stem all the way back to childhood, but the relationships look pretty different. Where I met Kimi in the isolated bubble of summer camp, I met Elle at our local public high school.

I knew about Elle before we ever had a conversation. Everyone in town knew about Elle. She was the class valedictorian and the captain of the drill team. She was a National Merit Scholar and on the homecoming court. She was strikingly beautiful, funny, and a church youth leader. So you can see why everyone knew her name, her face, and her achievements.

When we were formally introduced, I was just fifteen and a sophomore in high school while Elle was starting her senior year. She was laid up in the hospital, and I tagged along with a mutual friend for visiting hours. (That mutual friend, by the way, was Meg, who I write about as my Password Protector.)

I was intimidated by Elle and have no idea why she struck up a friendship with me. I was so much younger and didn't even have my driver's license yet. But what I do remember is that we immediately made each other laugh. As I write more about my Life Council, I can see humor as the most important common denominator in my close friendships. I can be serious by nature, so obviously I'm attracted to people who lighten me up. Elle was no exception. Her wit was too much for our town, really.

Even though I was younger and had my own set of friends in my grade, I started hanging out with Elle and Meg and their friends that year. They'd sneak me off campus for lunch, which wasn't allowed, and we'd spend hours driving around town in circles, listening to music and cruising slowly by the houses of boys we liked. Once we skipped school altogether and drove to Oklahoma City to audition to be extras in the Hollywood film *Twister* starring Bill Paxton and Helen Hunt. Believe me when I say we looked like quintessential Oklahomans, but somehow, we weren't chosen to be in any of the background scenes.

I knew early on that my friendship with Elle would go the distance. We were just weeks into our newfound friendship when we pulled out of Braum's ice cream drive-thru and my first lick sent my chocolate chip cookie dough scoop straight onto the floorboard of her white Pontiac Grand Am. Without a blink, Elle navigated the green stop light, reached over with one hand to the passenger side floor, and plopped the scoop— still completely intact—right back onto my waffle cone. She was a multitasker problem-solver with a concern for my snack. Who wouldn't be smitten?

I can admit now that I fell utterly and completely in love with Elle that year—not romantically, but the infatuation wasn't all that different. I drank in her every move and phrase. I wanted to be with her every spare moment. It made sense, given all her achievements and talent, but it was the first time I had a friend I wanted to model myself after, and I couldn't get enough of the high from being around someone so funny and smart. She was my first major girl crush, and it was intoxicating.

That first spring and summer after we met, we were inseparable, and even now I look back on that time as one that holds the best memories of teenagerdom for me. We had both started dating boys much older than us, and we'd all stay out too late at night in cars or out at the lake or creating small-town adventures, like driving to the woods to catch the sunrise. I knew even then that the time was fleeting, and when Elle left for college in the fall, I stood in the shower and wept like an abandoned lover.

I've thought a lot about that heartbreaking season of Elle leaving for college because it felt so different from any other friendship I'd ever had. Also, my feeling of being left behind in high school as she gained her independence in college almost assuredly contributed to what happened next.

While Elle and I had an unspoken spiritual bond that never wavered, we lacked the maturity to admit that we missed each other and that our age gap meant our lives were naturally going in different directions. We engaged in a series of major and minor hurts towards one another, the most egregious when I hooked up with a college boy who had hurt her enormously. I was stupid, and the whole situation was awful, and the fact that we were ever able to move forward at all is one of my life's greatest miracles.

Eventually I followed Elle to OU, and we mended fences after a few starts and stops because, the truth was, we were kind of addicted to each other. Our friendship chemistry was undeniable. She still makes me cry-laugh long before she ever gets to the punch line. God help us when we're at a social event together, because we always lock eyes and start laughing at the absolute most inappropriate moment.

Elle graduated from OU, went on to Duke Law School, and now holds a prestigious job. We go years without seeing one another, but she's one of my oldest and most important friends, and I know that she knows me in a way few people do. Like Kimi, Elle knows my most essential core self, but unlike Kimi, it's not because our friendship developed apart from our everyday context. The origins of my relationship with Elle are *rooted* in our everyday context.

We grew up in the same community, went to the same schools, attended the same churches, dated the same boys. Everything we say to one another has a subtext with history, whether it's an inside joke or a spiritual analysis. Elle knows my parents—they even hosted her wedding rehearsal dinner in their backyard—and she knows my siblings and all the backstories of our family. She understands every single implication of the way I grew up, a knowledge my husband and California friends will never get, no matter how precisely I explain it.

This is the value of an Old Friend, someone who knew you before you became the you that you are now. I can see why, after a lot of life change, some people want to shake off the friends who knew them before. But for me, being with Elle is like playing my favorite old mixtape. She is the song that was playing in my most formative moments. And no one else knows the words.

The Business Bestie

It doesn't matter if you're a teenager flippin' burgers, a stay-at-home parent running the house, or a CEO in the corner office, most of us enjoy our work more when we have a real connection with at least one coworker. And I'm using the term "coworker" here loosely because the "office" looks different than it used to. So while the traditional Business Bestie could be two cubicles over, I also consider this seat to be filled simply by someone in the same industry or in a similar role.

A Business Bestie is someone you can talk shop with, someone you can vent to about the boss, someone who will join you for a much-needed lunch break. The great benefit of a Business Bestie is that they understand your work world specifically, whether the particular politics of the company or just the challenges of your position. We spend such a large chunk of our day (and our lives) working, it is lonely and frustrating not to have someone who understands the dynamics of all those hours.

Here's the thing about a Business Bestie, though: they do not have to be a part of your personal life. They may or may not be someone you'd choose to spend time with on the weekends.

And it is more than okay to let that relationship stay right where it lives—at work.

I've been in a work friendship where we tried to hang out separate from the workplace, and it was just awkward. It wasn't that we liked one another any less; we just had less in common outside the office walls. I've also been in work friendships that transcended our jobs and became important, lifelong relationships, but it's not a requirement. I'm not even sure it's the norm.

Having a Business Bestie where you only discuss work and only see one another in a work context can be a healthy way to compartmentalize your professional and personal lives. It might also give you the freedom to be a different type of friend. For example, you might be more assertive or opinionated when speaking in a professional capacity than you are hanging out at a backyard BBQ with your Daily Duty Friend or vice versa. It might be easier or more comfortable for you to be able to embody your work self with your closest industry confidant.

But perhaps your job or personality doesn't require such considerations, and your Business Bestie is just the person who makes the time at work fly by. They're there for the latest office gossip and always save you a seat at the next meeting. Or, in my case, because my Business Besties are mostly work-at-home freelancers like I am, it's a relationship where we can discuss online strategy and the nuances of content creation that no one else in our lives understands or cares about.

I'm one of those weird internet people, someone who you can't quite put your finger on how exactly they make money, and I spend 98 percent of every work day in my own home office in a closet, alone. My personal story of Business Besties might be especially apt for those of us who work from home or who work on the internet, but I think it could apply to a wide swath of people, regardless of your business or your role.

From the time I was a newbie blogger to the rise of social media, I have relied on acquaintances doing similar work to show me the ropes. People working on the internet have been surprisingly forthcoming about strategies and ideas that work well for online business. Maybe because the nature of the internet means such tips will soon be obsolete, or maybe because those of us who labor in front of a screen are so desperate for real human interaction that talking shop totally counts as friendship, I've made dozens of online business friends who have been generous with their time and expertise.

I cannot tell you what a relief this has been. No one else in my real, daily life understands what I do all day. Not my spouse, my parents, my mom friends—no one. They don't get it, and I lack the patience and vocabulary to explain it to them. When your work is based on an ever-changing internet, it is a reassurance to talk to people who have the same frustrations with the algorithm or who want to troubleshoot their list-building strategy. I've been a part of groups that form naturally out of conferences or because someone puts together an email chain or Facebook group of similarly-minded people, and I have learned so much from these pop-up pods.

In 2018, I was invited to be part of a business-centered club with three other members, and that pairing of women has proved to be the most pivotal group of my online Business Besties. Jamie, Bri, Kendra, and I set out to be a "mastermind," a trendy term for a group of people who meet regularly and learn from one another. For me, the key difference from the beginning of this group, versus any other I'd been a part of, is that we were work-centered. The four of us were friendly, of course, and the three of them had a bit more friendship history together than I did with any of them, but we all wanted the same thing. We were serious about our work and craved a place where we could meet without the social etiquette of everyday friendships and without judgment that we were focused on one thing. We didn't want to talk about our personal lives for the most part, and we all had enough regular friends already. There was no pressure to present ourselves as having a healthy work/life balance and loving families and secure friendships and hobbies and homes and all the things that make up a full life. We assumed that we were each "whole" people outside of our occupations, and we accepted that our mastermind was a place that was compartmentalized for work alone.

We started meeting monthly online via video calls and soon added in a yearly in-person work retreat. As you might imagine, all this time together made us closer and aspects of our personal lives crept into the conversation. Five years into this mastermind, we can trust one another with something personal, but we also really respect it when one of us says, "I have this personal thing going on, so I need the distraction and want to talk about social media strategy for a while." Our careers matter deeply to all of us, so it's freeing to have a place where we can focus solely on that. At our meetings, I am just a podcaster or just an author, and I want to brainstorm and strategize without being expected to answer for any other parts of my life.

Another benefit to my Business Besties is that our friendship is structured. We meet once a month over Zoom, where we play the high/low game and each give a highlight of our current work life and then something we're struggling with. We help one another out where we can, or we just listen.

During our weekend work retreats, we each bring a project we're working on, and everyone gets a few hours of the whole group's attention to workshop their idea or problem. During those in-person weekends, we also share meals and have quiet work time and laugh. Of course, the conversations might turn personal. But they also might not. We're all okay with that. It's a boundary we respect and like.

Some personalities might take this compartmentalization as a barrier to closeness. For me, it provides the freedom to let my job and professional hopes and dreams stand alone. My longtime friends and my therapist may force me to talk about how my work goals fit into the puzzle of my life, but my mastermind is most interested in the plans for and execution of my job. Because of that sole focus, I have been able to move forward with more of my work dreams than I ever thought possible. It has been a huge mental encouragement for me as a solo freelancer to have this group of women cheering me on. We believe in each other's work. I don't have to convince my mastermind that what I'm doing is important, nor do I have to justify or explain why it matters to me. They care about me succeeding, which lets me care about succeeding without apology or explanation.

● ● ●

Jamie, Bri, and Kendra weren't my first Business Besties. Throughout my long and winding career, I've made a number of friends in the workplace that have become an important part of my life, but none so much as my friend Jennifer, a relationship that started with rejection.

My second job in Hollywood was working in film and television production on *jackass: the movie*, a big-screen adaptation of the juggernaut television show that has since spawned a million imitators (and four more movies). I took the job because having a feature film from Paramount on my tiny resume was a smart move, even if it meant a year of working far outside my wheelhouse. But even though I felt welcomed by the friendly cast and crew, and my own roommate was part of the production (see: The Battle Buddy), I wanted to establish closer friendships than those I had with the few acquaintances I'd met during my short time in Los Angeles.

While the crew was fairly male-dominated, I decided I should be friends with one of the post-production producers. Jennifer, who was a decade older than me and surely could not fathom why this just-out-of-the-sorority-house production assistant had plucked her out of the lineup, was having none of it. After I'd invited her to lunch with grand enthusiasm one too many times, she responded with a terse, "We are not friends. We are coworkers."

If someone said that to me now, as a forty-something woman, I would hear that message loud and clear and move on immediately. But as a naive and hopeful twenty-two-year-old, I thought Jennifer's declaration that we were only coworkers was hilarious, and I took it as a personal challenge. I guess that younger version of myself had the right attitude about that kind of a rejection, because my chirpy insistence that Jennifer and I hang out eventually worked. She rolled her eyes at me regularly, but we did, in fact, become friends over time. She had been working in the entertainment industry for years by that point, surrounded primarily by men, so maybe she couldn't resist a little female camaraderie, especially when it was all but forced upon her. Or maybe she saw, as I did, that we had more in common than one might think. We were both secret writers and made prayer a central part of our lives. The age gap between us was a bonus. She had a lot of wisdom about Hollywood that I needed, and I had a lot of energy and enthusiasm of the kind that had eroded in her after decades in a cutthroat environment.

Still, Jennifer and I didn't see each other outside of set or production-related social events. Even when I moved to her neighborhood for a year, we never met up for meals or mani-pedis. I was still squarely in the phase of life where I wore sparkly tops and went out to clubs, and she was more of a live theater kind of person, so it made sense that we confined our connection to work. After the movie we were working on ended, we both became crew for several seasons of a TV show where the production hours were long and the office drama unending. Jennifer was a respite from the chaos, and we turned to one another to vent or laugh about the temperamental personalities we worked with.

We were still coworkers and friends when I started dating our mutual boss, and in that tenuous work situation, she was one of the only people who supported our relationship becoming romantic. I'll admit there was a complicated dynamic on the crew before I left for another network, but where it would have been easy to get snarky, Jennifer chose to *believe the best* for me and Jeff.

Jennifer has continued to work with Jeff in the decades since she first resisted my friendship, and she remains an important part of our lives. She's a fixture at all of our family parties, and we're often one another's plus-one at literary and theater events we both enjoy. Jennifer has joined us for our annual Christmas Eve dinner for the last ten years and brings our kids gifts for their birthdays. If I'd let the matter drop at her declaration that "We are not friends. We are coworkers," I would have missed out on one of my best friends in this city, a friend who is now a part of our family.

I'm not saying you should pursue a friendship with someone who makes it clear it's unwanted, but perhaps don't be quick to give up on a connection with someone you have to see every day. They may be exactly who you need as more than "just a coworker." Even though our professional roles were very different, Jennifer became my Business Bestie when I desperately needed one, and our friendship stayed primarily at work for a long time. She didn't join us for the holidays until after we had kids, and Jeff and I were deliberate about the chosen family we wanted around us in that next stage of life. By then we'd known Jennifer for years, so it felt right to transition that professional relationship into something more like family. Other friendships from that same time period stayed at work, and that was okay, too.

Jennifer still works on many of Jeff's movie projects, and even though I've been out of the industry for a long time, we still talk a lot about work. With more than two decades of shared work history behind us, we now rarely have to explain the backstory on an issue or outline our thought process on a professional decision. The Business Bestie understands something about your work life that very few others do. I'm glad I bugged Jennifer to be friends, and I'm glad she finally gave in. It's a friendship that has given me life throughout some long, long days.

Your Business Bestie relationship might look different from mine. With Jennifer, I turned a coworker into a family friend. With my mastermind, I want work to dominate every conversation. Your Business Bestie might let you be personal in a work environment that's all business, or let you focus on professionalism when you need to escape the personal. But I encourage you to think of a Business Bestie as a relationship that has healthy limitations, is good for you and for your job, and deserves a seat on the Life Council.

The Fellow
Obsessive

We are all obsessed with something, right? Is there anything better than geeking out and talking ninety miles a minute with someone who is equally obsessed with that thing? It doesn't matter if what you're obsessed with is lowbrow or intellectual or incredibly niche. In fact, it's probably more exhilarating to talk to a Fellow Obsessive when no one else in your life "gets it."

I'm thinking about TV shows, a video game, a hobby, an Instagram account, celebrity gossip, cooking, a podcast, a sports team—whatever or whomever we're obsessed with at any given moment. When we're alone with that obsession, we might feel a little silly, yet when we find a Fellow Obsessive, we feel justified in how much we care about it. Meeting other people who are obsessed with the same things we're into is also a good way to make new friends. A shared passion starts off a friendship with something in common and gives you plenty to talk about.

I spy Fellow Obsessives around me all the time. There are

forums for popular reality shows, apps built around fitness trends and diets, membership groups for podcasts, fan fiction sites created around beloved book series, and more. I grew up in an area of the country obsessed with football and now live in an area of the country where basketball reigns supreme. In Hollywood, I'm also frequently immersed in conversations around movies and movie-making, and that in itself is a small world of obsessives.

For the record, I'm aware that some obsessions can go dark and shouldn't be championed. It might not be your personality or in your best interest to have the Fellow Obsessive on your Life Council. But kept in check in a healthy way, a shared obsession is a bonding experience. It can also be a way to add accountability to your life, whether that's to meet a goal or just make sure that an interest doesn't tip into dangerous territory.

Also? It's just fun.

My first real obsession started in elementary school when I stumbled across a book featuring newly taken photos of the *Titanic* underwater. I became fascinated by the tragedy and checked out everything available from the library on the topic. Learning about the *Titanic* kicked off a lifetime of interest in the macabre. By fourth grade, I'd discovered Stephen King novels, and my life has never been the same since. My neighbor's mom kept a shelf of Stephen King titles in a bookcase on the second floor of their nearly-one-hundred-year-old house. Ryen and I were in fourth grade when she showed me her mom's stash of horror novels, and I can point to that year as the one when my taste for dark stories really solidified. Ryen and I would pull down the well-worn paperbacks and flip through the pages until we came to an especially scary or naughty scene, and then we would dog-ear those passages for future reference.

I suppose it's developmentally natural for kids to be drawn to the forbidden, but our shared obsession with Stephen King became deeper than that. I can't imagine that our ten-year-old selves understood what any of those stories were really about, but Ryen and I were both voracious readers and both recognized the magic in King's words. Over and over, I read the opening passages of *It*, where Bill Denbrough's little brother, Georgie, chases the boat down the street and into the gutter encountering Pennywise the Clown. It was terrifying, yes, but it was also expertly crafted suspense, and an emotionally moving setup for the righteous fight the kids would engage in for the future of their small town.

Ryen and I pored over the copies of Stephen King while sitting cross-legged on her squeaky oak floors, and when we couldn't take it anymore, we'd go back to the safety and comfort of The Baby-Sitters Club and Sweet Valley High. No one else in the fourth grade seemed to like our scary taste or have access to those types of books. Ryen and I were both latchkey kids with working parents, so we were also given a level of independence that some of our classmates were not.

We found out quickly that we had to keep our Stephen King obsession quiet, lest someone ban us from reading his books. The clandestine nature of it added to the adventure. Would I have been too scared to read those stories if I hadn't had someone alongside me who was equally fascinated? We'll never know, but Stephen King has been my favorite author (worthy of my obsession) for over thirty years.

As I write this, I have a ten-year-old fourth grader at home, and it's impossible to predict which of his interests will stick, and which are being driven by what his friends are into or what the algorithm feeds his brain when he watches videos. What I do know is that my early obsession with Stephen King has been one of the more defined tastes of my life. All these decades later, I still claim King as my favorite author, and it's not based on nostalgia but in discovering my literary preferences with a friend reading alongside. Not many of my earliest obsessions made it out of childhood, but this one has, and becoming a superfan has been made exponentially better by knowing other fans (Fellow Obsessives) who are just as eager to discuss King's work as I am.

• • •

Conferences are a great place to meet Fellow Obsessives. Presumably you're all there because you care about the conference topic, which gives you an excuse to go full tilt into the obsession without having to temper yourself the way you would for the rest of society. Have you ever seen photos from fan conferences like Comic-Con? Attendees have the time of their lives wearing costumes and watching panels of their favorite characters, authors, actors, or experts on the thing they're obsessed with. Music festivals can feel the same way. I think sometimes these events get ridiculed because they're built around such specific worlds, but that's what makes them wonderful. While blogging and podcasting conferences have a slightly different flavor, I cannot tell you how fun it is to be surrounded by hundreds of people who are spending their free time toiling away behind a screen trying to create something, people who are encountering some of the same problems I'm having, people who are in the same industry and want to spend hours dissecting it as work or play.

If conferences are the in-person version of meeting over a shared obsession, there have long been online outlets for this, too. You can easily find Fellow Obsessives with just a few clicks. I'm in (at least) three different active Facebook groups tied to podcasts I listen to religiously, and I look to Reddit (not always a positive experience, to be honest) when I really need to feed my hunger for whatever new online controversy I can't get enough of.

If you're a parent, you're well aware of the different ways you can fall into baby forums where moms of all ages and philosophies will dispense advice and solidarity on every single aspect of your child's development. When I had little ones, some of the more popular groups were formed around the month and year your child was born, so not only were you communing with other mothers, you were communing with other mothers who had children born at exactly the same time as yours, which meant you were more or less in the trenches together for those first few years (see: The Battle Buddy).

Real-world and online options for Fellow Obsessives are plenty, with pros and cons depending on the level of your fixation, but how does this friend earn a seat on the Life Council? I'll admit that this one looks a little different due to its potential to be transient. I think it works best when it's a real-life someone you know rather than a faceless group of internet strangers. But I also think our obsessions can be mile markers of our lives. Unlike my lifetime love for Stephen King, many of the things we become fascinated with only stay with us for a season. Maybe it's for the duration of the TV series or current circumstances (like the baby years) or just until we lose interest and find something else to consume us. So when we look back at the years we were obsessed with different things—yoga or *The Bachelor* or true crime or TikTok—they become markers of that season.

My friend Jamie is my current favorite person to take an obsessive deep dive with (you may also remember her as one of my Business Besties). Jamie is a successful pop culture podcaster with a wealth of information on all kinds of things, and we can spend literally hours talking about some moment of internet culture from every angle possible. It is embarrassing, frankly, how many words and minutes we can give to social media minutiae. I would not subject anyone else in my life to the type of analysis we unfurl together while two time zones apart. With Jamie I'm able to get out all my thoughts, questions, and feelings about online drama with someone who understands the need to talk it to death.

Jamie holds this seat on the Life Council for me not only because I enjoy every second of our shared mania, but also because she holds me in check on our mutual obsessions. We can say to one another "Okay, we're too fixated on this," or steer one another back onto a higher road when we start to go low. We also frequently have different takes on whatever we're discussing, so we don't just provide an echo chamber for one another's opinions. We often manage to use the tidbit we're obsessing over to learn more about one another or to see another side of the topic.

When I was writing my first book, I drove out to Palm Springs to hole up in a hotel room for a few days and knock out a few chapters. It was still early in the writing process, and I was nervous about how it was going. On my second night in the desert, Jamie messaged me about some juicy Instagram content that was going viral, and even though it was two hours later in Alabama, I asked if I could call her on the phone.

We ended up talking for over an hour about the dumb post that was causing such an uproar, and then, maybe because it was late or because we were feeling especially connected, we pivoted to talking about some personal things that were happening in our offline lives. When we got off the phone hours later, I looked around my quiet hotel room and felt less lonely. The next morning, I woke up and was able to work on my book with less nerves, and I know it was because of the long conversation that left me feeling connected to someone I care about and who understands a side of me that not all of my friends do.

This is the power of the Fellow Obsessive. It can be a friendship of circumstance with someone who makes for a great companion, or it can be much more than that. My past and present Fellow Obsessives have made deep imprints in my life, and I've shared something with them that is rare and wonderful.

The Battle Buddy

The word *battle* might be a little dramatic, but I'm not taking the sentiment lightly. The Battle Buddy is someone who has a shared difficult experience, one you soldiered through together. It might be a personal journey—going through cancer treatments at the same time, for example—or it might be an adventure you were on together, such as being a part of the same rigorous degree program.

Having a buddy while you go through something hard is what makes the battle bearable. Like the Business Bestie, they understand something that likely no one else in your life does. The downside to having a Battle Buddy is, of course, that you had to go through the difficult thing at all.

The duration of the experience you share may vary. You may consider a coworker in a toxic work environment to be a form of a Battle Buddy, and that friendship may go on daily for years. Or, your version of a Battle Buddy might be someone who shares a special bond with you, even though the difficult event only lasted a single afternoon.

No matter your version of the "battle," the bond with a Battle Buddy is impossible to overstate. You might not share much in common beyond the hard thing that brought you together in the first place. Nor can you easily put into words what it feels like to have a witness to a traumatic period. Having a Battle Buddy brings relief and gratitude, anger and sadness.

The Battle Buddy fulfills a very specific role on your Life Council. While many of your friends or mentors will be able to give solid advice or be a listening ear, only the Battle Buddy can relate to the specific struggle you share. You might turn to your Battle Buddy for a long time after the metaphorical war has ended as someone who understands the residual effects that you're living through or who can see how far you've come.

Growth is even better with a witness. As we grow and evolve into better versions of ourselves, it is satisfying to have others notice, especially those who were by our side on those rocky roads. My Battle Buddy Amber has been my witness.

The first time I saw her, Amber was standing behind a podium in a Nashville ballroom, addressing several hundred women at a blog conference. She had a stylish pixie cut and a deep Southern drawl. I thought she was so pretty. And though I can see how Amber's friendliness might be described as approachable, I was immediately intimidated. Amber has command of herself; she has a presence. It was a time in my life when I felt lonely and small, so her confidence made me feel unworthy.

I didn't end up meeting Amber at the conference where I saw her speak, but that first impression stayed with me. We weren't formally introduced until the next year, when we wandered the halls of the same Nashville hotel at the same conference, and that time, both of us were pushing strollers with new babies.

Amber had been blogging longer than I had, and we approached the task of sharing ourselves on the internet from very different angles. She's a natural writer—her words seem to flow out of her as easily as her long arms and legs move with grace. She treated her work like the poetry it is, deciding to write and write and trusting that those who were meant to read it would find their way onto her path. I treated blogging more like a video game. I thought if you knew the right tricks and codes and tunnels, you'd eventually stumble upon a huge audience behind some secret wall. I was trying to game the algorithm before I even knew what that word meant. Amber had four little boys at home in Arkansas and a wild past. I had two babies in California where I was making up for lost time as a Goody Two-shoes. But there was a friendship spark right away.

Amber and I had dozens of friends in common when we met. Blogging friends, of course, but our worlds overlapped in other ways, too. We had mutual friends from college and summer camp and old churches. It felt as though, if we hadn't met at that blogging conference, we would have met some other way eventually.

After a few years of our friendship growing deeper and deeper online and offline, Amber and I were both invited on two different trips that cemented our relationship into the friendship hall of fame. The first was to Israel with a large group of esteemed and established writers among whom, frankly, I'm not sure I belonged. During our eight days in the Middle East, we toured historic biblical sites and various areas of war-torn Palestine. Our group was never in any direct danger on the trip, but it was an eye-opening experience both spiritually and politically.

I wanted to go to the Holy Land because I believe that God can speak to us through place. In my world, God had been silent for a while, so meeting him near Jerusalem felt like my best bet. I desperately wanted to hear answers to my long-standing prayers. I wanted something magical to happen that would make everything about my faith crisis make sense. While this trip was meant to be an educational one centered on the Israeli/Palestinian conflict, I was hoping for a personal spiritual nudge on the side.

Amber, too, was in a time of spiritual desperation, and together we were angsty, confused, and conflicted throughout our stay, often locking eyes across the room communicating our questions and disquiet. On one particularly long day, during the bus ride from one site to another, I started to have a full-blown panic attack. I've struggled with a lifetime of anxiety, and panic attacks are not uncommon for me, but this was an inopportune moment. We were on a full, enclosed bus, bumping along a road with the ceaseless drone of an educator coming over the speakers. I couldn't find quiet. I couldn't slow my breathing. My heart raced, and I stopped taking in air. If you've ever experienced or witnessed someone legitimately panicking, you know the crazed (or sometimes dazed) look that comes into their eyes.

As Israel's landscape raced by, the fatigue, overwhelm, and constant stimulation of the trip hit me all at once, and I thought I was going to come out of my skin there on the faux-velvet bus bench. Someone near me realized I was struggling and reached into her bag for the only helpful thing she could find, which turned out to be an orange essential oil. She passed it to Amber, who rubbed the oil generously on my wrist and instructed me to inhale deeply. When the attack eventually subsided, I looked across the aisle at Amber, who was staring back with a worried expression. She started to break into a loving, knowing smile, and something about her face meeting mine broke the spell. I went from panic to hysterical laughter, which she joined in a moment later. We cackled maniacally on that bus until we finally grew quiet together.

The year after we traveled to Israel, Amber and I were both invited on a trip to Haiti as guests of an organization we respected. This was a shorter trip, lasting less than a week, and I said yes because I thought it was important to use the platform I was building online to highlight good work being done around the world. My intentions were good, but looking back, there are a number of things about both trips that I wish I had done differently.

Haiti is breathtakingly beautiful, but the poverty is soul-shattering. It was jarring to go from my own country of abundance to one that needs so much. There were only five of us traveling this time, and Amber and I shared a room during our few days on the island. We would whisper long into the night about all we were taking in.

To share these perspective-changing travels with the same person puts Amber in the Battle Buddy category for me. In the last decade, Amber and I have shared rooms a number of times during getaway weekends and social gatherings, but those long nights abroad make our relationship unlike any other. The original group of blogging friends that brought Amber and me together is still intact, albeit with some changes over the years, and there's never a shortage of things to catch up on or personal events to analyze. However, I can't help but feel that Amber and I have some secret knowledge of the other because of the travel we've shared and the trajectory of change we've both been through spiritually.

Amber holds my heart without judgment, she'll speak truth to me when necessary, and she'll hold my hand through a panic attack. She has been a witness to my growth as I have been to hers. And we have the battle scars to prove it.

• • •

There is only one friend in all my forty-something years who witnessed in real time the most radical and redemptive season of my life thus far. Megan started out as a sorority sister who transferred colleges before we got to know one another. A few years later, word reached us through friends that we were both open for an adventure after graduation, and we both had the West Coast in mind. (For the record—and I know this can be a bit confusing—but Megan is a different person from my friend Meg who is mentioned throughout the book but especially featured as my Password Protector.)

Megan had family friends in Los Angeles and a deferred acceptance into medical school, so she was on more of a defined path than I was. I was drawn to LA—for all the glamorous reasons anyone is drawn there—but I knew no one, had no job opportunities, and was nursing a shattered heart that was keeping me from making clear decisions. What I did have clarity on, however, was a desire to escape my home state and reinvent myself. Megan had no such aspirations for reinvention, and thank the Lord there weren't two of us wandering and wounded. We moved into a light-filled apartment on Hollywood Boulevard in August 2001, and she became the steady, kind, thoughtful captain of our metaphorical ship.

I've written and spoken a lot about moving to Los Angeles

sight unseen when I was twenty-two because it has become a central part of my story. I've also spilled a lot of words about Megan over the years, since it is impossible to tell the story without mentioning her. But I've never really dug deep into what made our friendship so special and why Megan will always be the Battle Buddy from a year that changed us both forever.

We didn't have much reason to trust one another. She was on her way to being a doctor, while I wasn't consciously on my way anywhere. But we're both fairly quick studies with good heads on our shoulders. We knew just enough about one another to believe we'd each make rent and wouldn't party too hard, and honestly, at twenty-two, what more do you need?

Also, we didn't have any other options. Sometimes, when you're thrown into a situation, you just have to take a deep breath and hope for the best. There's simply a lot of luck involved when you're choosing a partner for a year or for your life. You can't always know how someone will act when they're in the trenches. You can't always know how *you* will act.

But I got lucky with Megan. She let me lie in bed and listen to love ballads and be sad. She drove me around in her green Jeep while we let the California sun warm our faces. We shared tube tops and cheap strip mall Chinese food and picked up one another from the airport at ungodly hours. This was years before smartphones or social media. For many months, we didn't have a TV in our apartment, so we spent untold hours sitting on her little white couch just talking. And talking. And talking. I swear all that talking started to heal me from the inside out. That and the California sun.

I limped along for those first few months of living with Megan, and she held me up as if I had an actual injury. We made some friends and went to bars and breakfast. September 11 happened, and we weathered the news cycle and our own fears together, absent family nearby.

Then, in the earliest days of 2002, Megan and I started working on the same film. I was a production assistant and spent most of my days answering phones at the front desk. Megan was a personal assistant to the man who would eventually become my husband. I want to laugh, shudder, and cry to think of what early 2000s Laura and Megan would think of the Laura and Megan of the 2020s. It would have felt impossible because it almost was impossible.

Megan and I working on *jackass: the movie* was, honestly, absurd. We were not suited to that particular brand of humor. We weren't qualified to have jobs on a movie set. And yet, somehow, it worked out. Megan had the luxury of letting it be a fun detour on her more respectable path, and I had the luxury of doing this crazy thing alongside a friend like Megan. Without her beside me at a job that required a lot of flexible judgment, I doubt I would have stuck around, and I wouldn't have the life that followed.

When Megan and I had been working for a few months, at just the time my broken heart was healing, the boy who had caused that broken heart turned up at our apartment. It wasn't wholly unexpected, as it's possible that during a late-night drunken phone call I might have invited him, but it was definitely a wrench in the flow of all that was becoming good that spring.

He brought a friend, and they crashed on the couch for a few days, and Megan stayed almost entirely out of our way except for the occasional raised eyebrows when she saw that a weaker, more subservient Laura seemed to be leaking out all over the apartment where a strong and determined Laura had once stood.

On the morning of his departure, after a weekend that had included more than one tearful argument and definitely one regrettable tattoo (him, not me), Megan and his friend left for a little while to give us space to say goodbye. He was sitting on our white couch with the sun coming through the windows when I came out of the bathroom in my towel, fresh from a shower. I was still entertaining the fantasy that he might leap to his feet and declare undying love, that the few days in LA had shown him what a wonderful life I was capable of building, and that he would suddenly want to be a part of it. But he didn't have a great poker face, and the truth was written all over it. He radiated mild irritation and possibly deep-seated jealousy, but nothing approaching love.

When Megan came back to the apartment, her face was wary. Her voice trailed off when she asked me how it went. And as I'd done for the last eight months we'd lived together, I poured it all out, and she just listened. The relationship that had so damaged me was now truly over, and I would be okay. Two truths she'd helped me learn.

At the end of our year of living together, Megan and I were both devastated by her departure from California to Georgia for med school. We were done shooting *jackass*, but we were still in post-production, and I was asked to take on her job as Jeff's assistant. Though Jeff and I already shared a connection by then, me stepping into that role definitely changed our futures.

Megan and I were in lockstep through the most transformational year of our lives. The adventure of moving to Los Angeles together without a plan, witnessing America change on that sunny September day, and the thousands of lessons that working together on a movie brought two Southern sorority girls gave Megan a grasp on who I am at my deepest core. Living together that year meant so much more than just sharing physical space. We ended up sharing all we had.

Megan fulfilled her dream of becoming a doctor. I married Jeff. We both became moms. We've never again lived in the same city and have only seen each other a handful of times since 2002, but every time we talk, I sense a deep knowing between us. We catch up on work and family and what's going on with mutual friends, but we never have to catch up on who we've become, even as we've both changed in the intervening decades. I believe that Megan and I saw all we needed to know about the other in just twelve months of a hard, enlightening year. We each know exactly who the other is, regardless of life's circumstances. I could call upon Megan for advice and trust that she would be objective about the facts but partial to me as a person. Just one intense year did that. And that is the value of a Battle Buddy.

The Yes Friend

This title might be unflattering—offensive even—if you equate the Yes Friend to the colloquial "Yes Man" that describes a weak person who is only capable of agreement. But a Yes Friend is *not* a Yes Man! Yes Friends aren't mindless or spineless as the "yes" may imply; rather, they are fun. They are spirited. They are often the life of the party. Their "Yes" comes from a place of adventure and enthusiasm, and the value they bring to our lives is pretty much unmatched.

Yes Friends are the ones most likely to pick up the phone, willing to grab a quick drink, and flexible when the plan changes. Yes Friends usually dislike conflict. They love making memories. Yes Friends are up for almost anything.

If you don't have a Yes Friend, ask yourself if *you* are the Yes Friend. Do you love being with people? Are you the social coordinator in your friend group? Do people often come to you for restaurant recommendations or travel advice? If so, please know that you are providing one of the best parts of friendship—fun.

The Yes Friends in my life have pulled me out of a funk when I'm down, dragged me out of the house when I was working too much, and made sure our girls' night out was at the best place with the right combination of personalities. Yes Friends are leaders. Their enthusiasm is contagious, and their energy can change the world.

Like almost every type of friend on the Life Council, the type of Yes Friend we want in our lives changes over time and in our different seasons as our definition of "adventure" evolves, but there is always such solidarity in having that person around who is a quick and easy yes to fun.

My esteem for the Yes Friend dramatically increased when I went to college. Before that, I didn't have much experience with Yes Friends. I was an introvert with a healthy high school social circle, but my Saturday nights were about as exciting as a movie marathon or trip to the Sonic drive-in, and not exactly the teenage party scene. There just wasn't a ton of opportunity to witness the joy of a big Yes. In college, I came across the ultimate Yes Friend and was immediately appreciative of the energy. An enthusiastic Yes personality can elevate a room or an event within minutes.

Shelley was my sorority sister, and she knew how to have a good time. That's not a weird college euphemism—although Shelley did have all kinds of college fun—but I mean she literally knew where the fun was. Before the days of regular mobile phone usage, Shelley had her pulse on the party, the vibe, how we should get there, and a backup plan in case it was a dud.

Shelley was available for a french fry run during a study break and could pack a travel bag in fifteen minutes flat if a weekend plan materialized. But here's the thing: Shelley may not be exactly what you are picturing. She wasn't loud. She wasn't the center of attention. If you scanned the room, looking for an authority figure or someone in the spotlight, you probably wouldn't land on Shelley. She fit in but she didn't stand out. She had big hair and a wide smile and was often dressed to the nines, but you'd have to be paying attention to understand what made everyone love Shelley.

One thing was her absolute consistency. If you wandered through a dorm room or sorority house hall, Shelley was around. If you felt uncomfortable at a party and just wanted to sit in a corner and chat with someone, Shelley was your girl. If you needed a ride or advice on a spot for dinner or a vote on if a dress looked better with heels or boots, Shelley had an answer.

During the weeks after college graduation, before I moved to Los Angeles, I was wallowing in that heartbreak that felt like it would swallow me whole. Our college town had been emptied of students and was sleepy and quiet in the hot Oklahoma sun. Shelley was one of my few friends who had stuck around to take summer classes. On the days I just couldn't stay in bed under the covers anymore, Shelley would show up at my apartment and take me to get a Dr. Pepper or something stronger. She had been hanging out with some boys we both knew and would drag me to their house near campus, with its overgrown lawn and faded hand-me-down furniture, and we would all watch movies together or sit outside on the porch and sip cheap drinks.

I was quiet in my sadness, so I listened more than I talked, and in those slow, sweaty nights, I could hear Shelley's care come to the surface. She flirted lightly with those boys, out of habit, I think, more than interest, to keep the mood high. She clapped along with their attempts at acoustic guitar and was gung-ho for whatever gross frozen food they made in their dingy kitchen. I wonder if she would have been hanging out with this patchwork of friends if she wasn't trying to keep me entertained during that sad summer. I still wonder if she knows that her insistence that we "go out" so much during that June and July was one of the only things that kept me upright.

Shelley was generous with her time and friendship, but I've often wondered if she felt taken advantage of since I was always on the receiving end and rarely reached out to her to make plans. I hope she knows how much I needed her in my life and that her presence taught me so much about being a friend to someone who is going through a hard time.

I lost touch with Shelley after college and have no idea what her adulthood looks like. But if I had to guess, I'd bet she's surrounded by friends. She's probably the PTA president and serves on the board of numerous charities who find her indispensable. If everyone wants a Yes Friend like Shelley when they're young, think how much more valuable a Yes Friend is as a grown-up.

●　●　●

My friend Tracy is the current Yes Friend who has made my life richer just by being her extroverted, exuberant self. I met Tracy a few months into the school year when my daughter started first grade. All the other moms with kids in first grade had been at the school for kindergarten and had already formed a tight-knit mom group. A death in our extended family meant that we were behind in a lot of ways—certainly in starting elementary school.

At the school Halloween carnival, I was overwhelmed and overstimulated by the chaos of two hundred kids and their sugar highs, and I was trying—nicely—to extricate myself from the whole event when Tracy came blazing up to me in the school gym to introduce herself. She exclaimed that she had been waiting to meet the new family. I was surprised that anyone would take notice of a new family in the crowd, but now I know that this piece of information never would have escaped Tracy's attention. She grew up in LA and seems to know everyone in the San Gabriel Valley. Our daughters were in the same grade, and soon enough they were in the same friend group, so as playdates and activities started to form around these very social six-year-olds, I got to see Tracy in action.

That year, I wasn't in the market for new friends. I was barely keeping my head above water with work and family following a few stressful years marked by loss and change. I had a handful of strong friendships and had convinced myself I didn't have the capacity for any more, and in a sense that was true. But sometimes, right when you decide you don't need something, it arrives at your door. Or rather, at your school carnival. I very much needed a Yes Friend like Tracy to bring some levity to my life.

Right away, Tracy was like a master class in how to do friendship. She calls or texts just to check in, and she does it with a regularity that has taught me something important about the maintenance of daily friendship, namely that it takes effort and thoughtfulness and can't be haphazard. Her social calendar is always jam-packed but she always wants to fit in one more thing and knows just the place to do it. In a city known for flakiness, Tracy never, ever cancels last-minute.

But as Tracy folded me into her mom friend groups, I stayed a little bit on the periphery. It was lovely to be included, but I was still hesitant. The women were friendly and funny. Their group texts were daily and chirpy, fun and helpful, yet I felt so jaded. I'd been living in Los Angeles for fifteen years, and a mom for over six of those years, and it had never been this easy. I was skeptical. Where had this band of women been for the last decade while I searched all over LA for connection?

One of the first things I noticed about these women—Tracy, especially—was their follow-through. This is a town rife with "We should get together!" and "Let's have lunch sometime!" With this new group, I had to start watching what I suggested, because Tracy would grab her phone and start naming dates and times and roping in anyone else we might want to invite. You couldn't toss out taking the kids to the park without Tracy pulling up a list of the best parks in the city, sending you a Google Maps address and then a Yelp review of the closest ice cream spot. Playdate planned! See you at 3 p.m.!

As I got used to it, I discovered this way of being in the world was thrilling. I eagerly reported back to Jeff all the things that Tracy had turned into a Yes, and suddenly—in a very short amount of time—I was becoming a Yes person, too. Yes to letting Lucy try Girl Scouts. Yes to a moms' night out. Yes to Palm Springs for a birthday party—you bring champagne and let's carpool. It was such a complete turnaround from the female friendships I'd had in LA up to that point. It felt like a whole new world. And it was anchored in Tracy.

Over the next several years, I traveled with Tracy more than I'd ever traveled with anyone outside my family. We flew to New York City, Deer Valley, New Orleans, Miami, London, Paris, and Amsterdam. We went to the desert and to our lake house. Tracy researches the best places to eat and buys tickets to the best activities months in advance. I happily tag along, so I'm not sure if that makes her or me the Yes Friend, but I know that I never (ever) would have gone on these trips without her.

I'd like to think that I'm a good friend to Tracy in ways

other than making dinner reservations. I bring my gifts of listening and affirming and cheering and, yes, showing up for her. Tracy sometimes bemoans always having to be the planner in our friend group, but she's also picky about where we eat and what we do, so it's mostly guaranteed that we'll all have a better time if we just let her handle the planning.

That said, it's important to recognize the work that goes into being the Yes Friend, the one who is always up for plans, whether making them or attending them. Whenever I talk about friendship online, I always end up hearing from a lot of women I suspect are probably Yes Friends who are frustrated that they're so often the coordinators, the initiators, the ones who have to rally everyone else to make the fun things happen. If you have a Yes Friend, take a moment to shoot her a quick thank-you. Send her a text, give her a hug, chip in for flowers if she's the one who planned the entire girls' trip. Your Yes Friend probably likes being a Yes person, but it's important to notice her and appreciate her time. If you *are* the Yes Friend, and if it feels like a never-ending thankless job, I hope this helped you reframe your enthusiasm for the gift that it is.

Where would the rest of us be without our Yes Friends? I know it wouldn't be as fun.

The Mentor

Of all the Life Council members, The Mentor is the seat on my council that has rarely been filled, and I feel that deficit. It's not that I don't have older, wiser, or more experienced women in my life who light the way. I do, and I'll share in this chapter about a few of those who have been important to me. But there is a certain type of mentor I've often longed for, the dedicated role of advice-giver, and I've never sought it out, even when it was especially needed professionally. I really could have benefited from an official mentor relationship in my twenties and thirties, and now that I'm in my forties, I believe I could be a valuable Mentor on a younger woman's Life Council. If you have (or are) a Mentor, consider yourself lucky.

Even though I haven't had a formal mentor, I've had many, many women who have taught me how to *be* just by allowing me to observe their lives and work practices. Some I've straight-up asked for advice or wisdom, and others I barely know at all but have still "mentored" me from afar—teaching me directly through their books or podcasts or teaching me indirectly as a member of my social circle or community.

Should it count to have someone you don't know well or at all on your Life Council? Well, yes and no. This is a book about friendship, which implies a interpersonal relationship. But if ever we were going to venture into the part of the conversation that examines the imbalanced relationships we have with some of our largest influences, it would be in discussing The Mentor. In the absence of having a real-life friend in this role, virtual teachings from the likes of Oprah and Brené Brown are better than nothing.

Still, my wish for both of us is a traditional mentor to sit on our Life Councils, someone who can guide and advise and keep tabs on us in real time. I can't overstate the importance of the women who have directed me on my path in some way, even in an unofficial capacity.

When Cyndi first met me, I imagine she was rather suspicious. And she had the right to be. I was fresh out of college, brimming with youth and enthusiasm, I had landed in Los Angeles without a job or a friend or a plan, and I showed up on her doorstep unannounced in all my hopeful naivete.

Cyndi's husband, Trey, was a family friend of my new LA roommate Megan (see: The Battle Buddy) and also a television network executive tasked with finding Megan and me entry-level jobs in the industry. So that we could make some money in the meantime, he offered up babysitting for his and Cyndi's toddler, housesitting when they traveled, and the only social invitations on our calendar was to their house for dinner or to Sunday breakfast. Cyndi, meanwhile, was juggling the baby, a successful and time-consuming business, and an ongoing home renovation. I imagine that behind closed doors, she questioned the appropriateness of two college-aged girls suddenly becoming part of their daily family orbit. There was truly nothing untoward about the situation, but I didn't fully grasp until much later how it might have looked.

To her credit, Cyndi took on Megan and me like the family friends and mooches we were. As an LA native, she modeled California casual in every way. Cyndi taught us where to shop for good food and cool clothes and quirky housewares. She taught us how to throw together a last-minute chic dinner party and how to stay cool when meeting a celebrity. Megan and I flagrantly copied Cyndi's style and envied her seeming ability to do it all and wondered aloud to one another if our futures could look anything like hers, post-baby and mid-career. Cyndi was effortlessly aspirational.

I can see now that Cyndi was one of the first women in my life who openly and directly said "This is how you do this," not because she's bossy (she's not), but because I asked. Something about the way our relationship was set up from the get-go—with her and Trey verbally and logistically taking us under their wings as an actual favor—gave me the freedom to pepper her with questions about how to handle everything from bikini waxes to how to order wine at dinner. It was also Cyndi's personality to answer generously. She had no pretension. There was no hidden motivation. She didn't ask to take on two young adults as mentees, but she did so with heart and gusto.

During that first year in Los Angeles, Cyndi once paid me for my babysitting with designer jeans. She knew that if she paid me cash—which she'd been doing, well above the going rate—I would force myself to save it or use it on something useful. She also knew I wanted the popular jeans at the time, going for a hundred dollars a pop, and that I would never splurge on them for myself. So she hauled me to the mall, we rode the escalator up to the second floor of Bloomingdale's, and she let me have my pick of any denim in the store. I must have tried on twenty pairs before I found the exact style that was both trendy and classic and with the little label I had been drooling over on the pocket. That shopping excursion might not have meant much to her, but to me it was thoughtful, observant, and wildly out-of-the-box. That was the other thing Cyndi offered me over and over again: she thought differently from anyone else I knew, and I desperately wanted to think differently from what I'd always known.

By that point in my life, I had admired or emulated multiple women, but it was always a passive relationship. I observed them, I did as they did, but it would have felt tacky, immature, or uncouth to ask them about their philosophies or processes. I was raised that it was simply expected that a young woman understood how to be (and how *not* to be, I suppose), so it was enlightening to ask Cyndi about her ways, especially since her West Coast attitude was such a contrast to all I had previously known. As one of the first people I got to know after moving to Los Angeles, Cyndi remains one of the largest influences on my entire life. A decade after meeting her, I did have a baby, and I did know the perfect girlfriend gift to buy, and I did throw candlelit dinner parties in my backyard—all the things she taught me about. Cyndi was a glimpse into what I wanted my future to be, and she showed me exactly how to be once I arrived there. I owe her enormously. (And I still have those jeans.)

●　●　●

Years after that entrenched season with Cyndi, after I'd already had my first baby, after I'd left one career and started another, I met Chris Ann because she (literally) chased me down a hotel hallway to take a photo of my dress.

I was at a blogging conference–that same one where I'd met Battle Buddy Amber–an event teeming with smart, driven, well-dressed women, so it was quite a compliment that Chris Ann tracked me down as I was entering the grand ballroom. She snapped my photo, and we got to talking about our blogs and the conference, and she instantly made me laugh. She was more than a decade older than me (but then again, so are my sister and my husband, so in that sense, age isn't always the Mentor factor you might expect), and we connected instantly.

Chris Ann and I are alike in some important ways: both creative, ambitious, and a little flighty. We both care about style and are quick to laugh. We're verbal processors and often don't even know how we feel about something until it comes out of our mouths. We have similar spirits, and we recognized something familiar in one another.

But we are different in many ways, too. Chris Ann has four kids, all older than mine. She lives in Minnesota. When we met, she was just launching her online home decor business with her best friend, which would eventually expand into a brick-and-mortar store.

She was at that conference in 2010 to learn more about online marketing and the technical aspect of her retail shop. I was there for creative inspiration and to get a handle on best practices for becoming a "real" writer. So Chris Ann and I weren't exactly in the same business, and the age gap alone wasn't enough to make her a Mentor to me. That lightbulb moment came on a different weekend.

The next year, we both showed up at the same conference again, and it was there that a group of internet friends formed.

These seventeen women entered my orbit after years of lone-liness. We created a communal friendship that taught me so much about carrying one another through tough times and celebrating with one another in the little things and not just the big ones. We functioned primarily in a private Facebook group, but after we'd been chatting in that forum daily for six months or so, we decided an in-person retreat was necessary in order to take our friendship to the next level. I offered up my lake house in South Carolina as a free and friendly desti-nation, and what followed was the start of an annual weekend of girlfriends who otherwise communicate solely through a screen. It was such an example of the way women's friendships were beginning to evolve thanks to the internet.

In that first year together at the lake house, Chris Ann and I were standing in the kitchen waiting for the oven to heat up—or maybe we were waiting to take something out of the oven—and we got into a conversation about marriage. Not everyone in our internet friend group was married, and no one else had a marriage that looked like mine from the outside. Jeff and I had only been married a handful of years at that point, and even though I was fully aware of his great passion for his career, I was still struggling with the dynamics of having two babies at home and a co-parent who was gone a lot of the time.

Chris Ann's husband was in a different industry but also worked a lot, and much of it included travel. She had twice as many kids as I did but was familiar with the power struggle of a spouse who works long hours and a mom attempting to be a professional creative. We stayed in the kitchen talking for hours, long after whatever was meant to be in the oven was cooked and served. She said some things out loud that I'd barely ever let myself think, let alone speak. She understood feeling resentful while not wanting to appear ungrateful. She verbalized the tension of being in a traditional marriage that was inherently patriarchal while also wanting to raise empowered daughters. She talked about holding down the fort solo, unending weariness, and the luxury of having a successful spouse, which allowed us to chase our low-paying passions.

I wanted to weep at all that Chris Ann saw in me and at the mixed feelings about my marriage and motherhood that were tearing me apart. She had such wisdom and grace, she didn't think less of me or of Jeff, and she had sage advice for how to take care of myself and my family along what she knew was a long road ahead.

In just one conversation, Chris Ann became a mentor to me. There were many factors that made talking about my marriage with anyone who wouldn't understand off-limits. Eventually, I got over my fear of talking about some of these topics with other friends, but when I met Chris Ann, I was so deep in the weeds of my own shame spiral (not to mention the hormones and sleep deprivation and everything else that comes with new motherhood) that it took making a friend in similar circumstances who was willing to name out loud the issues I was struggling with to help me see that I wasn't completely alone in my feelings.

That was over ten years ago, and Chris Ann is still my go-to for marriage and motherhood advice. She has stayed open-hearted and wise towards me, and as her children are young adults now, there's nothing she hasn't seen as a seasoned mom. Also, unlike me, she holds life a little lighter, and while I can get deep in despair and self-criticism, Chris Ann is quicker to laugh and offer a broader perspective. She sees through a wide-angle lens when I can't see what's possibly next.

It was Chris Ann who first explained the idea of the Life Council. When she described it as a friend version of a Board of Directors, something clicked in me regarding how to think about my various friendships. With Chris Ann's permission, I started working on this book, and now I'm realizing that maybe there are more Mentors in my life than I ever gave credit to.

They aren't the type of Mentor I'd pictured in the beginning of my career, when I was hungry to sit at the feet of a wizened guru who would usher me onto my path, but over the last few years, I have developed a few formal relationships that serve in a Mentor role. As I was launching my first book, I turned to a few author friends who were further down the publishing road and were happy to chat and offer advice. I also hired a business coach to help me figure out some of the logistical and emotional challenges of running an online business. This was a paid relationship, but it was mentor-like nonetheless. And although this isn't *my* family situation, I have many friends with deep relationships with older relatives or friends that I know they would describe as their Mentors.

Throughout this book, I'm asking you to rethink your friendships as a way to see the abundance and not the lack of relationships in your life. It's something I needed to do for myself as well. For so long, I've believed my own narrative about not having a Mentor, even though I knew it was an important seat on anyone's Life Council. But I *do* have figures who are there when I need them as advisors, even if they also fill other roles, even if they are paid, even if I only see them once a year or less. A "mentor" has a broader definition than

I could see at first, and it was a lesson for me to see my Life Council take shape in such a literal way with those who serve as actual counselors to me. I hope that as you're reading, your own Life Council is crystallizing and that any seats you've dismissed or secretly longed for will show themselves as having been filled all along.

The Password
Protector

The Password Protector is one of the Life Council members you may think you don't need, but I assure you, you do. In an analog world, the Password Protector has the key to your home, or your car, or your safe deposit box. She would race over to your house in the event of your untimely demise and burn all of your private journals with the messy thoughts that you would never want your spouse or children to read after your death. She would know just where you keep them: in the back of the closet, along with a shoebox of trinkets from your old high school boyfriend that no longer hold that much meaning to you but which you can't bring yourself to throw away. Again, not something you would want any member of your family sorting through without supervision, so the Password Protector is expected to perform this Herculean task, even if grief or appropriateness gives her pause. It takes a certain type of personality and a closeness you can trust, even from the Great Beyond.

In today's world, though, the Password Protector is a

little more literal. She holds your actual passwords. To your laptop, to your social media accounts, to the Google doc with the half-finished novel you've been tinkering with for years. There's a practicality to this type of friend—presumably, if you're incapacitated in some way, someone might need access to aspects of your digital life—but there's also an emotional safety in knowing someone out there has your back if you're ever unable to handle your business.

Now, before someone shrieks at me that you should never, ever, under any circumstances ever, give out your actual passwords to anyone in this world, let's take a deep breath of cybersecurity. Be smart about the person to whom you entrust this sacred information. Please do not give out actual passwords to anyone who has anything to gain personally from knowing them. Please do not give out passwords that have anything to do with your money. Banks and other financial institutions have processes in place that allow for emergencies. In some cases, social media platforms allow you to designate someone else on the platform to post from your account in a crisis situation, which does not require the actual transference of passwords but simply gives someone access. If this whole thing is making you itch, then take this Life Council member simply as a metaphor for a deeply trusted individual.

For me, though, this seat on my Life Council is literal. When I was in college, one of my best friends read my journal. At the time, my primary journal was a Word document on my laptop that I accidentally left in the study hall of our shared residence one day, so she might initially be forgiven for stumbling across the document without knowing exactly what she was reading—except for the fact that it would have been clear within a few sentences that what was written on the screen was deeply personal and, also, I was known for keeping a journal, so the most obvious thing to do (when reading a personal piece of writing on another person's laptop that you have no business poking around on) would have been to slam the computer shut and pretend it never happened. Right? Well, what this person chose to do was *write a reply at the end of the entry.*

That's right. After this friend consumed my rather lengthy, weepy, and self-pitying journal entry about how I felt unloved and worthless and all those other types of feelings that one works out about themselves on the page they think no one will ever possibly read, she chose to type an encouraging message back to me, as if we were in a dialogue.

I was mortified and infuriated and, since that time, I have remained hesitant to journal on a computer, opting instead to keep my most private thoughts in an old-fashioned notebook, immediately recognizable as a diary of sorts. This method doesn't keep it safe from being read by someone else, but at least then a person would know from the outset that they were breaking a boundary and couldn't claim—as my college friend did—that they were ignorant what the document actually was.

For a long time, that was the only breach of trust I knew of in my decades of journaling, though recently my mom confessed to reading my journals when I was a teenager. Philosophically, I do not love this, but as a mother of a teenager myself, I understand it.

Since I've been journaling for such a long time, I have stacks of old journals. I do not believe a person has to keep old journals—if it's cathartic to you to throw away your own thoughts from painful seasons, then by all means, burn those things to the ground—but I have kept most of mine. They feel precious to me, and I am tender towards the words my younger self wrote down on those lined pages of yellowed notebooks. But when I was writing my first book, I hauled some of them out of the rickety trunk where they live, and it was clear that no one, in the event of my passing, would care about or even decipher what was on those pages. The context is lost, sometimes even to me.

For this reason, I do not have a burning desire to keep those old notebooks "password protected," if you will, unlike my friend Meg, who has a dedicated local friend with very specific instructions for dealing with her journals in an emergency.

Even though we think about the journal thing differently, Meg is my ultimate Password Protector. Meg and I have been friends since high school, when we consecutively dated the same boys and declared ourselves sworn enemies until we both decided to ditch the boys and be friends instead—a good decision, indeed, since our friendship has now lasted longer than almost any other relationship in our lives.

If you must know the juicy details, I dated Meg's high school sweetheart, Todd, in the immediate aftermath of their drama-filled breakup. She was a beautiful, talented, charming junior, and I was a scrawny, near-sighted, nerdy freshman, so the love triangle was baffling to anyone with better eyesight than me, which was everyone. Meg was rightfully furious at my encroachment on her freshly single ex, and she retaliated by making out heavily with *my* recent heartbreak and first love, Clint, who promptly became infatuated with her. In time, Todd broke it off with me, and Meg promised to stop kissing Clint, and once we were both free of the entanglement, it was clear that we had more than just the boys in common. We became fast friends and remain on one another's Life Councils to this day.

Though she could fill numerous spots on the metaphorical Life Council, I'm classifying Meg as my Password Protector because she literally is. Meg has access to my social media accounts and has the password to my website platform. I gave her these encrypted codes because we are almost exactly the same degree of tech savvy, and we generally agree on "how to be" on the internet. This is no small thing. If you ask a dozen friends what is appropriate or wise internet behavior, you will get a dozen and a half answers. So if you find a friend who appears to have the same internal rules about what to share and how to share it, cling tightly to that person and name them your Password Protector.

Across the fifteen hundred miles and two time zones that separate us, Meg and I operate online almost completely in sync, although she is two years older than I am and two years ahead of me digitally. She started a blog a year or so before me. She started a secret internet group of friends and invited me to tag along, as usual. She started a podcast—and asked me to be part of the cohost team—and eventually I spun off and started my own show. She wrote a book, and then I wrote a book. Okay, so maybe it seems like I'm just copying her at every turn—which I am—but believe me when I say she's blazing a trail and I'm happily following her. We also have the same ideas about what we can and should do on the internet, and it's been a constant topic of discussion between us for a dozen years now.

Before I officially deemed her my Life Council Password Protector, Meg demonstrated her skills in real time. In the opening hours of motherhood for me, I was thrown into an online situation that I still cringe over. The whole thing was my fault, but it's a lesson I continue to learn from.

My daughter, Lucy, was born in the fall of 2009, and I was deep into my digital photo obsession. (I remain deep in my digital photo obsession.) I had a Flickr account, which was then just a place to upload and share photos. This was long before there were so many ways to digitally organize photos and before most of us fully grasped the issue of privacy and security online.

I had created a folder in my Flickr account to share new baby photos with far-flung family and friends, and one of the benefits was that sharing through Flickr required only a private link to the folder. Grandparents didn't have to sign up for a service or input any passwords to view the photo gallery. I thought I had covered the bases with the security preferences I'd checked for my account, but it was a rude awakening when I learned otherwise.

The email came in while I was sitting at the pediatrician's office with a brand-new baby cradled against my milk-stained sweatshirt. I was having trouble breastfeeding, my delivery wounds were still fresh, and I was exhausted and hormonal. Staring up at me from my phone was a notification from a blog reader—a stranger to me—who wanted me to know that the link to my private Flickr photo folder had been shared in a fan forum dedicated to my husband's movies. The thoughtful reader could tell by the nature of the photos that this was not meant to be shared publicly, and she wanted to alert me woman-to-woman that a change in privacy settings was probably necessary.

Her words, "the nature of the photos" was a kind way to say, "Girl, your post-birth boobs are all over the internet."

Pure panic ensued. The Flickr photo album I'd created didn't contain anything unsafe for family consumption, but I hadn't bothered to overly curate them, either. There were lots of hospital pics, which included images of me in the aftermath of an emergency blood transfusion. They were meant to give our extended family members a real peek into the adventure of Lucy's arrival earthside, and while they weren't full-blown nudes, they were certainly not intended to be seen by anyone outside of a very small circle.

The concerned blog reader (I thank the Lord for her discernment and also her careful wording of the situation at hand) was also part of an online chat room with thousands of members who were *jackass* fans. I have no idea where they got it, but someone had posted the link to my Flickr photo album in a celebratory way—congratulating us on the birth of our daughter. I don't think they meant to expose me cruelly. It was a different time online. But exposed I was.

In the doctor's office that day, I was consumed with shame and embarrassment, and for the life of me, I could not figure out how to fix it in that moment. I didn't know if I needed to go into Flickr; I didn't know if I needed to find the fan forum. Between the chapped nipples on my body and the nearly exposed nipples being passed around online, I simply could not think straight.

So I called Meg. Even in 2009, calling someone was crisis-level behavior, so it's no wonder she picked up. I quickly explained the situation and gave her my Flickr password right over the phone, then I told her to handle it and hung up.

By the time Lucy and I got home from the doctor, shaky and fragile, Meg had emailed me a detailed description of what she'd done. The settings, the deletions, and the details are lost to me now, but I was filled with such immense relief and also so secure in the fact that I had decided to call the exact right person in the exact right moment.

It never crossed my mind to change that password now that I'd given it to her. On the contrary, after that, I made a detailed list of *all* my important online passwords and sent it to her (safely) in case anything similar should ever happen again. I trusted her completely. I still do.

We all need some version of a Password Protector. Think about who you trust implicitly with your most important information: your passwords. Think about who shares similar online values. Think about what accounts would need to be accessed if something happened to you.

If you're hesitant to hand out actual passwords, there are numerous ways to handle this safely and securely. I have a file in my office that is sealed and signed and a file on my computer that I update regularly. My husband and Meg know it's there and that it contains some important instructions about my accounts. There are also services that offer this.

We all have a digital footprint that might require access in the event of an emergency. Think through what your personal needs are and attend to this task ASAP. Your Password Protector might also be your Business Bestie or your Soul Sister. This is one seat on the Life Council where the title doesn't matter so much, but the security and designation does.

The Empty Chair

We cannot talk about building and maintaining friendships without talking about the fact that some friendships end. This is a pain point that comes up time and time again, because eventually all of us will have stepped away from a relationship or be broken up with as a friend or lose a friend through circumstances beyond anyone's control.

I do not believe our culture gives enough attention to the pain of a friendship ending. Friends, after all, are seen as abundant. Replaceable. Shifting friendships are viewed as being as natural as the passing of time. But I've talked to women who mourned the loss of a close friend more than they grieved the end of a marriage. I've talked to women who, years after the fact, are still heartbroken and confused over whatever misunderstanding led to the end of a friendship, and remain bereft because it didn't seem to warrant a final conversation or explanation. I've even heard from women who have ended a friendship over something that seemed significant at the time, but who regretted the decision once it became clear that friendship chemistry isn't so easy to find again.

I've been there. I've chosen to end a friendship that was complicated, and I've been unceremoniously dumped by a friend I thought I would grow old with. Both of those situations happened a long time ago, but I still think about each of those women regularly and wonder if I should have done something differently. Recently, I experienced the fading of several friendships that I know were the results of natural evolution, and yet it still stings a little that none of us fought more for something that was once special.

This chapter isn't about an official seat on the Life Council; it's about the lack of one. It's the Empty Chair—the space that is there for all of us, whether we like it or not. Your attitude concerning the Empty Chair matters. You can see it as a seat representing reverence for a relationship that meant something sacred to you, one you're not quite ready to let go of, or you can see it as a seat waiting to be filled by someone important who has yet to arrive in your life. It is a memorial, or it is hope. Maybe it's both.

In the early 2000s, I was drowning. I felt quite progressive at the time, speaking candidly with friends about my mental health before it was so accepted, and I shared with others all the time (maybe overshared, to be honest) about the fact that I suffered from lifelong anxiety, that I pulled my hair out compulsively, and that I had various sensory issues. It was freedom to be able to be so open and still feel loved and accepted. I wanted to believe I was educating those around me and defying taboos, but I also think I was tying my anxiety too closely to my identity. I worked hard to portray my struggles as something interesting about myself instead of something that would require anything from others. Keeping help and concern at arm's length made me feel strong, even when I desperately could have used some intervention. It was the beginning of a terrible pattern that persists to this day.

So when depression hit—and it was such a radically different mental health struggle than my anxiety—I didn't know how to handle it at all. I couldn't bear to change the narrative that I could take care of myself. I put one foot in front of the other and just survived. I lost whole weeks to a near-blackout mode of getting through the day. There are pictures from that time that I have no recollection of taking. I know now that young adult mental health struggles are common, especially among those who already have a tendency towards them, but it's hard to see that when everyone around you seems like they're having the time of their lives.

My depression lasted for the better part of a year, and around the time the fog started to lift, one of my dearest friends was entering her own darkness. The details of her struggle were different from mine, but watching her descent panicked me. I'd only just broken the surface of my own hard season, and it felt detrimental to stay in the proximity of hers. Maybe it was. We have all kinds of metaphors about taking care of ourselves first lest we lose our own ability to function. One message I learned in church about temptation really stuck with me: the image of a person standing on a chair and reaching down to someone below them. How much easier it was, they preached, to get pulled off that chair than it was to pull someone up beside you.

I am filled with shame that I chose to end a friendship because I couldn't handle what my friend was going through. In my generous moments, I will acknowledge that sometimes, yes, you really do have to put on your own oxygen mask first. In my less generous moments, I worry I took the easy way out instead of being the steadfast friend I'd like to believe I am.

All we can do with our regrettable pasts is learn from them how to do things better the next time. That friend from whom I took such a deliberate step back has gone on to have a beautiful life, judging by her social media, where we are still connected even though we haven't been in touch for many years. I still feel a twinge when her face shows up in my feed, because I know I could have done better back then and that I have been trying to redeem myself ever since with the friends who came after.

•   •   •

Another important friendship ended just a few years later, and its ending was not my decision. It was one of my life's greatest heartbreaks, and it came not from a romantic relationship but from the dramatic demise of a best friendship. I can't even recount to you now exactly what happened, if I ever really knew. I had some theories in the months and years after it ended, and I have some different theories after years of therapy and some mature hindsight, but I guess it doesn't really matter. Our lives took different directions, and she decided to end our friendship after years of memories and laughter and holding that very specific label: best friend.

The end was definitive, which I suppose was a gift. I wrote her a letter and asked some questions about our friendship status, and she replied via an email that was just a few sentences long and with unambiguous finality. I've spoken to so many people about friendships which ended with them simply being cut off or ignored without any explanation, and how this is such a particular kind of pain, so at least I'm grateful (I guess?) that I didn't have to live in a state of wondering.

That friendship breakup wrecked me, although not at

first. In the beginning, I was angry and self-righteous, and when I talked about her and us, I always painted myself as the good guy or the victim. But after six months or so, I was in agony. I was long married, but that friendship breakup was indeed harder than most of my romantic endings. I cried a lot. I hid away our photos and visible memories, but it didn't stop my thoughts. So many things reminded me of her or of an inside joke. There would be breaking pop culture news, and I'd immediately want to text her about it until I remembered I couldn't. It pained me when her birthday rolled around, and the first Christmas when we didn't exchange family cards nearly put me in a fetal position.

Worse, there really wasn't anyone who, I felt, could understand my pain. My husband listened patiently, but our friendship had been long-distance as long as he'd known us, so he didn't understand all the history and intricacies of it. Mutual friends had seen how complicated the relationship had become in the final years, so they were sympathetic to my sadness but also believed it to be for the best. Unless you've gone through one, you can't imagine how much a friendship breakup can consume you.

Six years after I opened that last email, I was standing in a Target when a graphic T-shirt on display triggered a memory of that former best friend. And for the first time in a long time, I didn't wince or shove the thought away. I actually smiled, remembering something about this person who is so funny and who taught me so much about life in the years that we were close. It was a surprise to feel warmth instead of tightness in my chest. I took a moment to wish her well in my heart, and then I went on with my errands. That, I decided, is what healing feels like.

• • •

The other side of The Empty Chair is filled not with the pain of a past friendship but with longing for a friendship you want. The main message of this book is to take stock of the relationships in your life and what they bring to your table as a motivation to nurture them, but I know there are often gaps in our hearts if we don't have an Old Friend or a Soul Sister or anyone who comes close.

Just acknowledging that we don't have the exact friendship we want by giving a nod to that Empty Chair can be enough inspiration to start putting effort into seeking the friendships we desire.

When I lost my best friend, I didn't become friendless. There were other women I was close to who stepped up in the aftermath of that relationship ending. Even then, I had a very informal Life Council. But I kept an Empty Chair in my heart for a long time. In the beginning, I was in denial. Then I moved into the stage where I romanticized our friendship and thought no one else could ever fill her role. Eventually, enough time passed that I noticed the seats at my table were occupied. I'd made new friends and committed more deeply to some old ones. I wasn't consciously trying to replace the friend I'd lost, but the gaps filled, nonetheless.

On my Life Council right now, I keep an Empty Chair not as a memorial for someone in my past, but as a welcoming spot for friends in my future. As I make new connections and strengthen many of my relationships, I want space for them.

The Empty Chair on the Life Council isn't a seat to focus on, but it's a seat, nonetheless. I couldn't write a book about the value of friendships without recognizing how many of us are holding space for someone who once was or a hope for someone to come. Whether you're in the grieving stage or the hopeful stage, let the Empty Chair do its work and remind you of what is available at your table.

The New Friend

The thrill of making a new friend is very much akin to the thrill of early love. The chemistry! The possibility! At any age, it's fun to discover the spark of connection with someone. But the benefits of new friends are deeper than just the novelty or the ego. While long-term friendships can keep you grounded and remind you of where you came from, new relationships can shine a light on who you are *now* and how far you've come.

Still, many people will go a long time without making any new friends. If you're in a stretch or season where your life doesn't change much—same town, same job, same church, same activities—then the opportunity simply might not present itself that often. Others really don't have a choice. If you've moved to a different location or changed jobs or experienced other life changes, you either have to make new friends or be alone. This is where the Empty Chair from the previous chapter comes in. You have an Empty Chair you're willing to fill, and you're on the lookout for a New Friend with her own Empty Chair.

Then there's the fact that making new friends is sort of

terrifying. Again, as with dating, there's some risk involved. Some vulnerability. It might not work out. You may feel stupid or rejected. You may have to extract yourself from a possible new friendship that isn't quite working.

The New Friend takes the most effort of all the seats on the Life Council. Even if a fresh friendship feels easy, you're still constantly learning about one another and figuring out communication styles. It can be exhilarating, and it can also be exhausting. We're going to talk more about the logistics of making new friends in Part 3, but remember that attitude is everything at the beginning of a relationship. Your positive energy has the power to attract new people into your life, but the inverse is also true. If you wall yourself off to new friends, you probably won't make any. But stick with me here, because new friends are vastly underrated. Old friends get all the glory, but new friends can change your life.

We loved the Montessori preschool we chose for our children. It was a fluke, actually, that we ended up in the small school on a nondescript street in an unfamiliar neighborhood in Los Angeles. We applied one summer in a panic after our two-year-old daughter's application was rejected by the popular preschool in our area. We'd been told her admission was a sure thing. As it turned out, it was a fortuitous reroute for a few reasons, not the least of which was the educational path it launched our kids on and the social world it opened up for us as parents.

I had been told that my loneliness would be cured once I had kids. Everyone assured me that the sheer number of opportunities for mommy friends would abound once I was carting around a stroller and a diaper bag. But no matter how many Mommy and Me music classes or park activities I signed up for, I was years into parenthood before I made any real friends through my kiddos. Oh sure, I met people—we did occasionally get invited to toddler birthday parties and playdates—and the social calendar was lovely, but it wasn't leading to the deep friendships of my dreams. I can't pinpoint why, exactly; even now I think back on some of those acquaintanceships and wonder why they never went beyond the most surface-level chitchat. I'm pretty sure it must have had something to do with the mommy brain fog, the frazzled state, the fatigue. All of us were drowning a little bit. Swapping some stories and sharing goldfish crackers was about the best we could do at the time, and I have all the grace in the world for that.

When our daughter started at the preschool, I was pleasantly surprised to meet multiple women who were friendly and welcoming, and it was nice to see the same faces every morning at drop-off and every afternoon at pickup. Those brief interactions each day weren't exactly soul-fulfilling, but the consistency was sweet. A reason to put on a cute shirt and some lip gloss, at least. Sometimes just a daily friendly exchange can go a long way (see: The Daily Duty Friend).

We'd been at the preschool for a couple of years with our daughter, Lucy, when it was time for two-year-old Finch to start the program. The first day of the year at any school, things are abuzz, and everyone is nervous and excited. The hubbub was no different on this day. The front steps of the school were crowded with overeager, hovering parents, my husband and me included. Across the schoolyard, I spied a woman so familiar to me that I was just sure she was an established Montessori mom like I was, and I threw my arms open and went in for a welcome-back-how-was-your-summer hug. I was mid-squeal and mid-embrace when I noticed her startled face and my brain registered that I did not, in fact, know this woman at all. She was so familiar to me because she was the star of a popular television show.

Jenna *the actress* looks exactly like Jenna *the mom*, and her warmth in person is even more palpable, so much so that I mistook her for someone I already knew. This is not a completely uncommon occurrence in Los Angeles, where familiar faces abound, but never has it led to such an awkward beginning to such a beautiful friendship.

Our sons became fast friends in preschool, and so did we. Jenna and I have a lot in common: we read, watch, and listen to a lot of the same stuff, we have one son and one daughter each, we have similar ideas about work/life balance, and, perhaps most importantly, we both grew up in the middle of the country and not on either of the coasts. There are a lot of things about our lives that look very different from the outside, but I believe we're drawn to one another's general grounded-ness, a trait that can be hard to find in Hollywood. (We also share the ability to laugh at even calling ourselves "grounded." Everything is relative.)

When Jenna and I had been friends for about six months, she invited Jeff and me to be guests at her table at a charity event. This was in the spring of 2016, and my own lifelong conservative politics were taking a fairly wide swing left. This change was discombobulating for me, and was seeping into every aspect of my life, including my social interactions. That evening I got into a rowdy conversation with a few other attendees about the tumultuous political landscape in America, and in the valet line afterward, I cried silent tears at the confusion I felt about leaving behind a belief system

I'd been raised with and clung to for more than a decade of living in liberal Los Angeles. As a new friend, Jenna knew none of this about me, and she was naturally curious about my emotions at the dinner. This sparked several talks between us, and I realized that a new friend is so much more likely to let you change. She didn't hold or even know about my past political baggage. She let me talk it through as yet another way to get to know me, not to hold me to an old identity. I didn't have to unpack it all for her if I didn't want to. I could simply say, "This is what I believe now. This is where I have landed on this," and she accepted that because she knew no other version of me than the one standing right in front of her.

As my friendship with Jenna progressed, we moved out of new friendship into just solid friendship. We've been friends for seven years and counting, and we're still discovering new things about one another. Our boys are long out of preschool, but we share interests in podcasting and writing, and we still talk about things in our lives that people "back home" don't get. Her voice is a comfort to me, and she is wildly, hysterically funny.

Jenna graciously wrote the foreword for my first book, and on publication day in the middle of the pandemic, we both wore ridiculously dressy gowns and stood on her porch with champagne and took selfies six feet apart. There was such a long stretch of my adulthood when I couldn't imagine marking the most important occasions of my life with anyone except an Old Friend. But Jenna taught me that the gift of a New Friend is that they know you as the person you have become. And toast to it.

● ● ●

Coincidentally, I also met Patty on a first day of school. There was no awkward hug, though—more like awkward eye contact. My daughter had left the preschool and was the new girl in first grade, in a class full of students who had all been in class together for kindergarten. The sweet, smiley teacher pulled Patty and her daughter over to the cubbies where Lucy and I were standing with wide, overwhelmed eyes, and introduced us.

Patty and I both had our hands resting protectively on our six-year-old girls' shoulders, and we eyed one another skeptically. My conscious thought was, "This woman will never be friends with me." Patty is stunningly gorgeous, and she stood in that first-grade classroom at eight in the morning with long, stylish bangs and a form-fitting outfit that somehow communicated that she had a lot more interesting things to do with her day than babysit these latecomers. I was intimidated.

Besides, it's not like I wanted a new friend. I had put a lot of effort into finding peace with the friendships in my life. I was no longer lonely like I'd been in early motherhood, because I'd cobbled together a patchwork of friendships that were fulfilling and fun, from my monthly book club to my fellow mommy bloggers, to Jenna and the other preschool moms. It wasn't as cohesive and mimosa-filled as pop culture portrays adult women friendships, but I had regular and deep relationships with women I really loved. I didn't dare hope for more.

So meeting Patty in the first grade classroom felt perfunctory. I'd like to think I'd dropped the air of desperation that used to accompany every new female introduction.

But then a funny thing happened. The teacher sat Lucy and Patty's daughter next to one another that first morning, and a week or so later, they started asking for playdates with each other. Patty was already a social butterfly at the school and was quick to include my daughter in every activity. Before long, I'd been introduced to dozens of other first-grade moms. I was fielding more social invitations in that first month than I'd gotten in years. Patty was there every time, raising her beautiful wrist to wave me over, patting the chair next to her, making sure I knew everyone else at the table. My face would flush red every time this happened. I was so unused to being the New Friend in a circle that I'd forgotten how, if I'd ever known. I'd spent so many years trying to forge my own connections and being the one making overtures to others that I was struck shy and embarrassed at first to have people take an interest in me or our family.

A large part of what was happening was the parent culture of the elementary school. It was very social, and participation was expected. Looking back now, I wish I'd put myself in places before then where that was the vibe—through a church, work, or volunteer environment—rather than spending so much effort trying to create my own thing all the time. Believe me, plopping myself, however inadvertently, into a culture with a social calendar was so much easier than starting from scratch over and over and over again.

There was no denying that Patty was a hub of this activity, and as a New Friend, she saw me with some clarity that had escaped my own attention. She and the other women were meeting thirty-six-year-old Laura, established writer and podcaster, mom of two, secure-ish in her style and taste, comfortable with the fact that she didn't know everything, years into a therapy journey of healing and growing. Whenever I mentioned certain parts of my past in conversation— anything from my childhood in Oklahoma to my wandering days of working in TV and film—they were shocked or entertained. Some of those old stories didn't square with the Laura they were getting to know. They couldn't imagine it, but they also didn't judge it. They liked the only Laura they knew—the current version.

I cannot tell you how freeing this was. I didn't realize how apologetic I had become until I didn't have to be anymore. As I had changed belief systems and political parties and ideas about God and parenthood and money and all the things that morph and shift in a lifetime, I spent a lot of energy online and in person with old friends and family, assuring them that I was still the same person they'd always known. My undertone was that I was sorry I had let the world change me. My underlying plea was to still be loved. When I made friends who didn't require any such explanation for why I was the way I was, it was an enormous relief. I didn't realize how heavy it had become to carry the weight of others' expectations.

As a social ringleader and native Angeleno, Patty showed me parts of Los Angeles I hadn't embraced yet because I'd had no door to them. I'd lived in LA for fifteen years at that point, and still often felt like an observer. But Patty and her friends were glamorous and a bit "woo-woo," sending me to an energy healer, then to the latest workout craze and later detouring into a meaningful conversation about how our past traumas inform our parenting styles.

It was months before Patty and my new mom friends discovered my online work and social media channels. I'd purposefully kept these to myself, and I cringed when someone mentioned that they'd come across them. For the most part, I'd kept my online life and my "real" life separate from the beginning. This stemmed from my mommy blogging days, when it was considered smart to keep your real name and details off your own blog, but it was even more deeply fueled by the shame I carried from being "an internet person" for so long. When I first started sharing my life online, I was years into a period of loneliness and secretly found it a little lame that the only way I could have friends was through the internet. I'd also faced a lot of judgment from old friends and acquaintances for my "little internet pursuits," so I'd developed the habit of downplaying how active I was online.

Patty herself wasn't very active online and didn't pretend to understand that whole part of my life or why I kept it a secret, but she cheered it on, nonetheless. Once, when I pseudo-apologized for the fact that I had to self-promote my podcast on my Instagram account, she looked at me blankly and asked, "Well, how else are we supposed to know about it?" A friend seeing my posts not as self-promotional but as informational was a lightbulb moment for me and highlighted just how unsupportive some of my past relationships had been in this area.

To be fair, I get what's potentially awkward and cringe-worthy about someone you know trying something new and maybe not being good at it, especially when whatever it is they're trying is public. When I started blogging, it was definitely still considered nerdy and maybe tacky, and it would be years before social media and selfies were mainstream. Objectively, I can see where some people struggled with this "weird" thing I was doing on the internet in the beginning. Still, it was nice to meet friends who weren't witnessing me in the early days of a transformation. One can appreciate the bones of the "before," but it's nice to bask in the "after."

This is the value of New Friends and why they deserve a seat on your Life Council. They're not carrying the baggage of your past selves. They might hear a story about your old life, but they're getting to know you a little wiser.

When I met Patty, I still had my guard up a little. I was hiding my job and keeping in-person connection at arm's length lest I get hurt by a friendship that didn't work out. But after a bit, I began to relax into my skin in this new friendship and enjoyed getting to know someone with a radically different upbringing and with a generous spirit towards me.

You may feel hesitant about making new friends because you don't share any history or because it seems like a lot of work to forge a friendship with someone new or because your Life Council is already full. But don't skip this one. Don't miss out on what a New Friend can teach you about who you have become.

The Soul Sister

The Soul Sister is the only member of the Life Council that, in a perfect world, has a seat at the table forever. She is the Supreme Court Justice of the Life Council. Reverend Soul Sister. She wields a whole different level of power in your friendships because your connection is that intangible. You meet one another on a soul level. It's chemistry. It's a *knowing*.

You may be hesitant to claim someone as a Soul Sister because it feels a little too much like crowning someone BFF, and as full-grown adults, we should be past such labels. You may not even want to read this chapter because the idea of having a Soul Sister—a platonic soulmate—is something that has eluded you your whole life, and it's a tender topic. If this is the case for you, you're not alone. If someone doesn't immediately come to mind when you read about this Life Council member, take heart. You just haven't found her yet.

A Soul Sister can also be a Daily Duty Friend or a Business Bestie or a Fellow Obsessive, or she might just be her own thing. For me, the Soul Sister bond is spiritual. Our relationship just operates on a different level. When we are together, we are communing spirit-to-spirit somehow, like a vibration.

We have a foundation of understanding that sometimes comes with the length of the relationship, but can also just come with recognizing ourselves in each other. My Soul Sisters both happen to be Old Friends, but that's not a requirement for this role. The Soul Sister might be fully independent of any of your other friendships or wider social circle. She may exist outside of all that.

One of the Soul Sisters I'm going to share with you has never seen me be a parent to my kids. The other one has a personality so unlike mine that our gravitation towards one another doesn't make sense, let alone seem like it would last for a lifetime. Both of these friendships exist outside of my daily life. Also, I would jump in front of a train for either of these women, neither of whom has ever met the other one. Like I said, it's a special seat.

While a Soul Sister is inherently a magical relationship, it can still have its ups and down. We are all human, after all. Life circumstances change, and people's capacity for this depth of feeling may fluctuate. But what makes a Soul Sister stand apart is the lifetime appointment. You may go months or even years out of regular touch with a Soul Sister, but when you inevitably come back together, that innate connection remains.

Finally, the Soul Sister friendship has to be a two-way street. You can't have one person thinking you have a cosmic connection and another who considers it a just-for-a-season relationship. That imbalance would make the friendship something else. The Soul Sister dynamic is not always perfect, but it is always mutually agreed upon. It's also rare. So if you already have this spot filled on your Life Council, give yourself a moment to feel gratitude. If you haven't met your Soul Sister yet, keep the light on for her to find you.

There's a story from ninth or tenth grade that my Soul Sister Cara and I both remember vividly as a defining moment in our lives, not to mention the most pivotal moment in our friendship. We were on the cheerleading bus, going to an out-of-town football game. Cara and I were sitting together, as usual, our pale teenage legs stuck to the dark green vinyl bus seat that had grown hot in the Oklahoma fall weather.

The bus was full of girls in the same polyester skirts and high ponytails. In the handful of seats around me and Cara, they were draped over one another to lean into our heated conversation, not even disguising that they were trying to eavesdrop.

We were arguing about hell.

Specifically, we were arguing about the nature of God sending people to hell. It was an unsophisticated theology we were espousing, but we were both passionate about our positions. Cara was raised in a church home that boldly and regularly claimed that anyone who was not in their very specific denomination was headed for hell. Eternal damnation. A fiery forever.

I didn't believe in hell. My nondenominational Bible church didn't preach much about the afterlife, but also, I grew up in a family full of nonbelievers, so the idea of walking streets of gold while they sat in Satan's firepit didn't make any sense to me, so I rejected it entirely.

Since it's almost impossible to discuss the nature and consequence of one thing if the other party doesn't even believe in that thing, you'd think the whole argument would be a nonstarter. But Cara and I had been close friends for years before that day on the bus, and we loved one another and respected each other's opinions enough to keep trudging through, over and over, as a way to try to understand where the other person was coming from. The other girls on the bus were listening to us. Somehow, we had their teenage attention for a theology debate between two blonde-haired, sensitive souls who had exactly zero experience or knowledge outside their own community.

The big moment came when I used our handwriting as a metaphor. I loved a metaphor even then, and this one came flying out of my mouth before I had a chance to think it all the way through. The gist of this new angle was that even though I write my "A's" with one big loop and a stick on the side and Cara wrote her "A's" like the fancy typewriter font, we were both writing "A's." If everyone else could read the word in spite of our varied handwriting, surely God himself could see how we were both right on not just hell, but on everything. In writing our "A's" (living out what we believed), our intentions were the same, and the output was the same. It looked different, but it was a letter in a word in a sentence just the same.

This is a simple concept, and it also shouldn't be taken as a blanket statement on every disagreement ever, but there's no other way to describe the silence that followed my impassioned speech except as a watershed moment.

It was the '90s. We had no internet. We hadn't yet been exposed to many ideas outside of our homes and churches except for those of one another. So even considering that we might *both* be right on the concept of hell, or at least not be eternally wrong, felt like a Big Idea.

Now, solidly in our 40s and having gone through 475 belief shifts EACH over the last few decades, Cara and I laugh at our teenage selves trying to solve the world's problems on the cheerleading bus. But the truth is, it was a radical moment for us, both individually and as friends.

Cara and I existed in a tight circle of close friends throughout high school and stayed in touch loosely when we attended different colleges. She became a surgeon. I moved out to Hollywood. She was always "one of my best friends from home," but I cannot pinpoint when she went from Old Friend status to a Soul Sister seat, though it might have had something to do with the little vacations we started taking together, just the two of us.

They started as long weekends in our early thirties. We'd meet somewhere in the middle between my home in Los Angeles and hers in Oklahoma. In between delicious meals and walks and shopping and spa treatments, we'd spend hours and hours (truly hundreds of hours) talking about everything. The further apart our lives got, the closer we became. With almost every other friendship in my life, the opposite is true. The more you grow apart, the more you grow apart, but Cara and I did the opposite. We realized, as life got more complicated, that we thought about things almost exactly the same way, always. We took trendy personality typing tests and always ended up with the same results.

While Cara and I have all the benefits of old friends who met in the fifth grade—a shared history, similar background, same hometown, knowledge of each other's families and trajectories and all of that—there is also another ingredient that is much harder to define. We "get" one another on a soul level. We can make eye contact and, with absolutely zero expression on our faces, know exactly what the other person is thinking. I think I could confess murder to Cara, and she would nod sagely.

It's not because we had an instant connection when we met. We didn't. We were less alike when we were young. It's also not because we have put in the time, although we have. Cara understands me and how I think and how I make decisions, and we trust one another completely. I would trust her with my children. I would trust her with my money. I would trust her to operate on anyone I love without a second thought. But trust alone does not make a Soul Sister. We all know people we trust implicitly because they've proven themselves to be trust*worthy*, but they're still not Soul Sisters.

Cara and I are Soul Sisters because our souls are so much alike. I don't have many friends who understand exactly what I'm saying without much explanation, but Cara fills in the holes in my theories before I can even flesh them out myself. When my judgment is off about something, she's one of the few people who can call me out for it, and I'll listen immediately. I joke around that, as a surgeon, Cara is saving lives daily while I am futzing around on the internet, but we're actually operating from a similar core self, even though our professions are different.

We might never have known that if not for an argument about eternity on the cheerleading bus. And we might never have had that fight if we didn't each, on a spiritual level, trust where the other was coming from and that we would still be friends when our disagreement was over. So maybe a Soul Sister is about trust after all.

● ● ●

To this moment, I do not know why my Soul Sister Lindsay even likes me. Really. On paper, I am not her type. I am nerdy. I am a know-it-all. I am a stick-in-the-mud at parties. I barely ever listen to music, which is her greatest passion. It makes absolutely no sense that we would be even casual friends, let alone soul mates.

But I know exactly why I like her. It's not because she's the most fun person I've ever been around, or that she shines from the stage when she sings, or because everyone who meets her wants to be her best friend, although all of those things are true. I love Lindsay because, together, we laugh until we cry and we dance until we can't breathe and because, when we met at eighteen years old, she saw exactly who I was and she labeled us a duo and she hasn't let go of that title for a single second since 1997. To be attached to someone so ferociously has an intoxicating power, and now that we live 2000 miles away from one another after being roommates during our most formative years, I don't take that type of attachment lightly. I have been Laura of "Lindsay and Laura" for nearly three decades, and I hope it's always so.

Lindsay and I first came to live with one another in the dorms at the University of Oklahoma our freshman year, a roommate setup through family friends that has been one of the greatest gifts of my life. We lived in that tiny little shared space and, by fluke, we pledged the same sorority, further binding us to one another as we attended every meeting and party and meal and event together during those months when you're away from home for the first time and trying on independence.

We were initially baffled by one another. I was a lot more introverted back then, and college life was overwhelming to me. I hid in the dorm room a lot and stayed in the corner at parties, with my shoulders hunched, sipping on Dr. Pepper. I watched Lindsay in total fascination. Everyone loved her. She is a magnetic light the whole room is drawn to, but somehow she always makes *you* feel special, like you're the most important person in the room. Lindsay would drag me out of the dorms to be social, and I would drag her home before sunrise. It was a symbiotic relationship.

College is a mess, of course, and our time there was filled with drama and reroutes and romance and missteps. Once, I had a fender bender while Lindsay was my passenger and I was driving barefoot, and she had to give me her flip-flops so I could talk to the police officer. Our senior year, we flew to Florida for the Orange Bowl, where we bedazzled Oklahoma Sooners T-shirts in the back of a rental car and slept hungover under some seats at the airport on the way home. We've made a lot of memories in twenty-five years. A lifetime of inside jokes.

I moved to Los Angeles after graduation and, less than a year later, so did Lindsay. It was an enormous relief to have her here with me in this big city, like a little bit of home had landed. Eventually, we moved in together again, to an amazing two-story townhouse under the Hollywood sign that we could barely afford but didn't dare pass up. A new lifetime of memories were made in that place. Because the twenties are a mess, too. At least, they were for us.

I was trying to make it as a writer, and Lindsay was trying to make it as a singer, and chasing your dreams is hard work even with your best friend by your side. Over and over again, we reassured one another that all the trade-offs we were making were worth it. The nontraditional careers. Marriage and kids nowhere in sight. Scraping by to make rent and using any leftover money for fun and not investment. It's a really particular way to be a young adult, and it would be a disaster to do it alone. I can't imagine surviving that time with a lesser friend. I think I would have given up.

Lindsay and I might have been on different paths, but we know one another like we know our own selves. I can read even the slightest twitch in her face. She knows what I'm going to say before I even walk in the room.

At an MTV wrap party the year after we moved in together in LA, I introduced Lindsay to one of my coworkers. He was the kindest, sweetest guy on the crew of a show we'd just finished up, and it was no surprise that he fell in love with her. Everyone falls in love with Lindsay a little bit. After a while, that coworker moved in, and I moved out on my own. The year after that, after making a secret pact that we would get engaged or get on with our lives without those slow-deciding men, Lindsay and I both got engaged and married within the same year.

Lindsay and her groom decided to move from Los Angeles to Nashville, and I sobbed so hard at their rehearsal dinner that I literally could not speak. (I think guests believed I was having a nervous breakdown, and to this day, I am ashamed that I wasn't able to give Lindsay the bridesmaid toast she deserved. I hope this homage makes up for it.) At that point, Lindsay and I had lived together on and off for nearly ten years and shared all of the most important seasons of our lives together. I couldn't imagine going forward into marriage and family without her close. But somehow, we have. Just like when we lived together in that townhouse in the Hollywood Hills, Lindsay is still singing, and I am still writing, and we still consider ourselves the most unlikely of duos.

Lindsay holds the other Soul Sister seat on my Life Council not only because of our shared history but because of a deeper connection that kept us drawn tightly together throughout that history. We get one another in a way I believe no one else does, maybe not even our husbands, maybe not even our own sisters. Jeff once said to me that no one lights me up like Lindsay does, that I glow in her presence. Once, during a dark season of my life, Jeff quietly suggested that I invite Lindsay for a visit. He was desperate for the light in my eyes to flicker again. Lindsay seemed like the most likely solution. Another time, I got a late-night call from *her* husband. "Will you come?" he asked. "Of course," I said.

The Soul Sister has the special distinction of being a combination of all of your most important friendships. She is likely an Old Friend, Battle Buddy, and Password Protector all in one. The connection is both concrete and spiritual. Time marches on and circumstances change, but the Soul Sister bond remains consistent. It is one of her best qualities.

PART III

What I've Learned About . . .

Making Friends

Whenever I talk about the angst of making new friends on my podcast or on social media, the comment always comes up that it is so hard to make new friends as an adult. So many of us seem to struggle with those early interactions that turn an acquaintance into a friend. We think if we just followed exact instructions, it would unlock the elusive perfect bestie. But there is no formula to make this happen. There are too many variables at play, including personality types, communication styles, relationship preferences, and the culture of your community. So this isn't a how-to section so much as a brainstorming session to broaden your mindset on making friends.

There are two things that regularly trip us up when we're on the hunt for new friends. The first is that we believe it should be easy. The right people will just fall into our path. The chemistry will be instant. Conversation will flow. If none of that happens organically, there's something wrong—something wrong with the friend or the group or, in the quiet corner of our brain, something wrong with *us*.

This thinking is misguided. It's a story we're telling

ourselves that stems from childhood wounds or past friendship hurts. When we decide—often too early—that a friendship or our position in a friendship group "isn't working," we give up and either return to the comfort of being alone or start looking for friendship elsewhere, and the whole exhausting and defeating cycle repeats. It's all built on the false idea that awesome friendships must contain an element of magic.

But here's the truth: *There is no Friendship Fairy.*

Your perfect friendship match is not going to fall from the sky. Finding friends takes effort and vulnerability and a willingness to let it look different than you might have imagined. Interactions might be stilted at first. You might have to hang out a few times before it feels comfortable. There might be some form of adult rejection, politely or otherwise, like Jennifer from the Business Bestie chapter, who informed me we were not friends but coworkers. There might be occasions when you're the one doing the rejecting if it's clear you're not a friendship fit.

I know this feels like a big groan. Who has time for that in our adult lives? Also, maybe you have a story or two that feels like you *were* granted a wish by a Friendship Fairy when you met a great friend, and it's hard to accept that that type of kismet is the exception and not the rule.

This brings me to the other thing that often trips us up when we're on the hunt for new friends: we start the search looking for a Best Friend Soul Mate. Our standards are incredibly high for adult relationships, and I get it. Especially if you've had a taste of what it feels like to have a Soul Sister, it becomes hard to settle for anything else. When I first moved to Los Angeles and had a hard time making friends, I'm sure part of it was because I wanted everyone to live up to the deep friendships I had in childhood and college. Anything else felt less than. But it wasn't fair to compare brand-new friends with those with whom I had a long history or a lot more in common. Looking back, I can see that I should have let those young LA friends be a bit more fun without heaping so much pressure onto them. I could have let them be Yes Friends.

We all want the kind of lifelong friendships we've seen portrayed in pop culture. And while there's nothing wrong with hoping for that type of connectedness, it holds us back from the gift of the friendships right in front of us. Even if they're not that deep or not meant to be forever.

ACCEPT THAT YOU ARE NOT FRIENDSHIP DATING FOR FRIENDSHIP MARRIAGE.

Accept that you are not friendship dating for friendship marriage. There are no vows. There is no The One. We don't have to choose or be chosen. Friendship is so much more expansive than that. We are looking for a variety of relationships in our lives—including identifying who is already there—and the fact that no two friendships will look exactly the same is a good thing. This is why we build a Life Council slowly over time. It helps us appreciate what each friend brings to our world and lets us strengthen the traits we bring to theirs. It takes the pressure off one person to be our Everything.

Still, there are some nuts and bolts to making new friends.

Three Guidelines for Making New Friends

1. Keep Your Eyes Open
Often, the best candidates for friendship are right in front of us. I'm all for taking action and seeking out like-minded

people to add to our circles, but before we start from scratch, let's see who is in our line of sight *right now*.

Who is in your world already as an acquaintance or coworker or neighbor who could be upgraded to friend? Look around at the next soccer weekend or backyard barbecue or company Zoom meeting and try to notice who might have something in common with you. A book peeking out of their bag? Earbuds in, listening to a popular podcast? T-shirt from a coffee shop you like? Or just a friendly glint in their eye that opens the door to a greeting, a quick connection, a passing compliment or comment that you noticed them.

Noticing is a huge part of relationships that gets overlooked in the beginning of friendships—or even in established ones. Our lives are busy, and we're going from one appointment to the next, we're juggling the volleyball tournament with the charity bake sale, and it becomes easy to brush past acquaintances with a friendly wave and not much more. I wonder what would happen if we took the time to really *notice* the people in our general orbit.

I'm thinking about people who are already in our lives peripherally. They're on the team roster. They're the spouse of a coworker. They're the neighbor who walks the dog at the same time every morning as we do. What if we didn't dismiss them because of some snap judgment we made long ago? Too often, we decide someone is not our friendship "type" because of something superficial. They're always dressed nicer (or messier) than we are. They're too chatty, or they never say a word. They live far across town or there's a significant age gap or, I don't know, we're not immediately drawn to them, so we dismiss their friendship potential.

What if we gave them a second look?

Since friendships are easier to spark when you have some kind of a surface connection in common, paying attention to those who are already in your life will make the following steps of building friendships easier. You already share a neighborhood, a workplace, the kids' school, or a faith tradition. Start there. It's harder to bust into a friendship group that's already thriving, so look for those who are standing on the edges of your life because they're busy or shy or new.

Think it sounds too simple? Take this week to look around at your circle of acquaintances and see someone with new eyes.

2. Let It Be Loose

If you do identify someone in your wider circle who might be a candidate for connection, just let it be loose. You're casting a wide net on purpose, so stop holding onto a certain outcome.

When my two kids were babies, I put so much effort into finding mom friends who would look like the stroller mafias I kept seeing online. I put together parties and park playdates and was a regular attendee at the toddler music classes. I can see now that I was doing all the right things—participating in activities, not waiting on a Friendship Fairy—but I also know that I was so desperate for adult interaction that I might have come off a little clingy and needy with women I'd just met. I have all the grace in the world for myself in that lonely season, but I wish I had taken a step back and realized that my eagerness might have seemed like pestering to equally exhausted and overwhelmed new moms.

Once I got a bit more sleep, I was able to lighten up. I invited women and their kids over to the house with less expectation that it was going to be the Best Playdate of All Time or that we were going to become the Best Group of Mom Friends Ever. My only hope was that it would be a nice few hours with some decent conversation that didn't revolve around breastfeeding. I kept it loose by letting those friendships develop—or not.

And they didn't.

I lost touch with every single woman I met during those baby days. I could beat myself up for not trying harder or for trying too hard. Or, I could just admit that early parenthood is a rough season, and it was lovely to have some occasional light companionship, but it wasn't going to progress beyond that. It took me awhile to get there, but that's how I choose to look at those years. Learning to loosen my grip and accept those relationships for what they were put me in a much better position to establish deeper friendships down the road, because I was willing to let them evolve without pressure and with gratitude. That Empty Chair on my Life Council stayed empty.

After years of having mom acquaintances, I was able to recognize the difference when a relationship with more weight came along, which it eventually did.

I understand that it's tricky to balance the effort of putting yourself out there with the directive to hold it all loosely, but it's possible to do both. In fact, that practice is about more than just friendships in your life. You can strangle anything to death if you hold it too tightly: your career, your marriage, your art, your relationships.

Giving everything that matters to you space to breathe is a skill for a lifetime.

3. Consistency Is Key

One of the hardest parts of friendship can be the rhythm of it. We know that repeated contact strengthens the bond, but how do we get that level of consistency in this busy world? In an article for *The Atlantic*, psychologist and author Adam Grant tells us, "On average, it takes 50 hours of interaction to go from acquaintance to friend and 200 hours to get to close friend." That's a lot of hours.

If you don't already work together or share some type of institution that meets regularly, like a church or club or sports team, then you just have to make it up. Pick a thing you'd be willing to do consistently, and then set it up as a recurring priority.

A book club
A knitting club
A wine night
A Saturday morning power walk through the
   neighborhood

This is why making new friends under the umbrella of an activity or club that already exists is the path of least resistance, especially for those of us who struggle to make the first friendship move and for those who may struggle with planning and follow-through. It is much easier for me to make friends with someone who always attends the same yoga class I do or who is always in the bleachers when our team plays, because that guarantees I'm going to see them again fairly soon without having to initiate over and over. We already share spots on one another's schedules.

Having a consistent event already on the calendar achieves a few things. First, it helps to build those hours that are so crucial to deepening friendships. Second, it takes the emotional energy out of deciding what to do together every time. There are only so many instances when you can grab coffee together or go shopping or even take a trip. And if you're not a natural planner or initiator, those things will just never end up happening. If there's an agreed-upon, regularly scheduled thing, half the battle is already won.

The other half of the battle is showing up. Whether you decide to meet once a week or once a month, you need to make every effort to be there. Sure, stuff comes up, but adults can't give unending chances to people when they've made the friendship date a priority and the other person has not. Keep your friend dates as faithfully as you would any other appointments.

Don't be spooked by the idea of consistency in friendships. Your definition of "consistent" can be broad. I only talk to my Old Friend Kimi a few times a year, yet she still holds one of the longest-running spots on my Life Council. Our idea of consistency is that we pick up when the other calls. Always. That direct communication between us is so rare that our unspoken rule is that we honor the effort.

We've talked about friendship being a to-do, but it also involves a certain level of commitment. You can't just check the friendship box once and call it good. Hopefully, the time you spend together building or maintaining a friendship will be life-giving and not a chore. This doesn't mean every hour will be perfect, but time together with friends—either New or Old—is an investment in your spirit. The time you put into making new friends pays you back tenfold.

Making Friends Online

Can you make real friends on the internet? The short answer is yes. The longer answer is that it takes a different sort of effort and attention.

Just a few short years ago, it was still considered unusual to meet up in real life with someone you met online, but this has become an accepted part of how we live our digital lives. Still, it's intimidating to make the first friendship move with a stranger on the other side of a screen, and there's no set etiquette or rules for how to do this well. Like friendships that start in person, there's a certain amount of luck, timing, and mood involved with making friends on the internet.

In the last ten years, I've met some of my closest friends online. But my situation isn't entirely normal, even as working from home has become more common. My work keeps me online almost every day, and the general message I'm preaching encourages sharing and showing up. I'm not only more proficient at navigating relationships through a screen, my public profiles give others the advantage of knowing more about me through my social media or podcasts. Because of this, the dear friends I've made on the internet are almost exclusively some type of modern-day colleague—they're writers or podcasters. We're doing the same type of work, and we can check out one another's personalities easily before we reach out to strike up a conversation.

For many people, though, this is not the case. You have your privacy settings locked down and your defenses up. We've all heard so many horror stories about people being scammed online that many of us are understandably leery of online friendships that seem too good to be true.

But the internet has made it easier than ever to meet people who share specific interests, which can be immediately bonding (see: The Fellow Obsessive). In multiple conversations I've hosted on social media about meeting friends online, the most common origin story for these friendships was being part of a dedicated group for a shared interest.

These groups can be about life circumstances (military spouses, infertility struggles, local communities), hobbies (running, reading, crafting), or "fandom" (official or unofficial groups formed for followers of bands, sports teams, podcasts, or TV shows). The platforms are varied and have changed over time—from the early chatrooms and message boards to Facebook and Meetup groups and paid communities to whatever trend comes next—but what they all have in common is a virtual gathering of people who care a lot about something very specific.

Sometimes that's all you need. I've heard story after story of women who found solidarity online in ways that would be hard to replicate with real life friends. People who understand exactly what you're struggling with or who are just as eager as you are to throw yourself into a passion. If you want to make online friends, start where your people are. Identify the thing you want to have in common with someone (your life circumstance, a struggle, a hobby, or a fandom) and join groups using social media platforms or apps or websites. Be active in the comments sections. If you have a lot of interaction with someone who seems similar to you, maybe the conversation moves to direct messages. Remember the guidelines for making friends: keep your eyes open, let it be loose, and consistency is key.

I believe online friends can stay online and fulfill a very specific purpose in your life, but I've also experienced them translating into real-world meetups where I've confirmed that the online chemistry was even more pronounced in person. The converse is also true: I've had many budding online friendships fizzle out with time or fade when an in-person meetup wasn't as much of a match as expected. That's okay, too. Just like friendships that start in person, online relationships have their hits and misses and only work for a season before it's time to move on.

It may take a lot of tries before you find a friendship online that feels meaningful. But don't automatically rule out this method for finding friends just because it hasn't worked for you in the past or you're theoretically uncomfortable with it. The internet changes the world every day. Let it change yours.

Being a Friend

Making new friends often feels like the biggest hurdle, but what about caring for the friendships we already have? I see plenty of suggestions for how to help a friend through a struggle, but I rarely see anyone talk about the regular maintenance of healthy, active friendships.

This is where I've misstepped in my own relationships, as I described in A Friendship Reckoning. I think I'm decent at showing up with a shoulder to cry on when someone is going through something hard, but when regular life is moving along, I have gotten complacent or become absent to some of my favorite people. I've learned there's maintenance involved with your close friends, even when life is ho-hum. *Especially* when life is ho-hum.

I have to remind myself daily of my first Friendship Philosophy: *Friendship is a to-do*. To the best of my ability, I try to make my actions match what's in my heart. Sometimes this feels like a chore, but friends should occupy a certain priority if you want to remain bonded. Most of us are busy adults with plenty of responsibilities, so I'm not trying to heap more shame onto your plate. Quick check-ins, warm smiles and hugs, including friends in your news and listening when they share theirs—the small things can go a long way.

The plethora of ways available for friends to communicate with one another can be a blessing and a curse. Texting is convenient, photos on social media are fun, and there are all kinds of interesting ways to stay in touch through videos and voice messages, but it can get overwhelming fast. I've been open about the anxiety I feel when I'm inundated with digital messages, and my inability to be constantly available on my phone has caused certain friendships to flounder. I've had to find the balance between managing my own mental health and being a good friend, and those two things don't always align. Transparency about this helps, since my friends know not to take it personally if I don't text back right away. There is no specific formula for how to manage communication in friendship, only that you *do* manage it in some way. So many of the friendship struggles I've experienced or observed boil down to a failure to communicate or a misunderstanding in communication.

It also helps to understand your own friendship values. Friendship values are different from the Friendship Philosophies in part I. The philosophies are general rules I've created for how I want to approach all of my relationships, and friendship values are what we believe matters about the individual people themselves. The philosophies help to guide *my* behavior, and the values focus on what I desire from the other person. You might think we all have the same friendship values, but they can vary more than you might expect.

Friendship Values

As you're making new friends or evaluating some of your existing relationships, ask yourself what you value most in a friendship.

Don't answer reflexively. Really think about what you want and need in both casual friendships and in Life Council members. Sometimes, we demand traits in our friends that we really don't want 100 percent of the time.

Trustworthiness? Sure. It's important to know that you can trust friends with your secrets, to keep their promises, to take care with your things and your kids/pets/home.

Loyalty? What does this mean in friendship? That they will stand by your side when the hard times come? That they will defend you to others when you're not around? That they will stay your friend come hell or high water? That you should always be included in a group invitation? Loyalty in friendship isn't always clear, and if this is a strong value for you, make sure you've communicated those expectations.

Honesty? How honest do you *really* want your friends to be? Unfiltered? Only when it's necessary? What if their honesty is about the person you're dating or the paint color you picked for your walls or your new haircut? Sometimes people should keep their "honesty" on the inside, since it's often subjective and based on personal taste. But when asked in earnest for an honest opinion (whether the topic matters much or not), I hope my friends can discern when to tell me the truth and when to let me figure it out on my own.

Would you end a friendship if it didn't tick all these value boxes? What about the friend who hates confrontation? Who is radically blunt or tells too many white lies? Who you wouldn't choose to house-sit because, well, their track record for keeping plants alive is less than stellar? What if *you are* that friend?

Of course, we want to have friends of fine character, and being a generally good person matters. But we all have our flaws, and, frankly, our preferences.

When I spent some time working through this on my own, examining what I really want in my friendships and not just the popular answers for what I *should* want in friendships, this is what I came up with:

- Assumption of good intent
- Fun
- Curious

Not the words you expected? Me neither, at first.

Assumption of good intent is huge for me. I wrote more about this in my first Friendship Philosophy, *believe the best*, because it is the foundation for a healthy friendship in my life. I need you to assume that I'm doing the best I can, and I will make the same assumption about you. I pledge not to jump to radical conclusions about your behavior or your silence or your feelings, and I expect you to do the same for me. Even in conflict resolution, which all friendships will have, we both have to approach it knowing that the other person has good intentions.

Fun isn't all that original when it comes to relationship values, but I crave people who balance my serious nature. I can be dark and angsty and critical, and I do well to surround myself with people who lighten me up. Deep conversations are my natural tendency, but I feel the most fulfilled when I come home from an evening of laughter. As my adulthood marches on, I've found that I am getting more fun than I used to be (yes, really), and I credit that to my attraction to fun and funny people.

Curiosity is a value I don't hear talked about much when it comes to friendship. As a young person, I wouldn't have thought to spell this out because, back then, the whole world was an adventure. As a midlife mom, this value has come into sharp clarity for me. I want my friends to be curious about the world in some way. I want them to read or travel or follow interesting people on Twitter or send me a new podcast series to listen to and discuss. I want to reciprocate with lots of questions and maybe share an *aha* moment. I've seen how easy it is to stay in one's bubble, and I actively resist that. I love it when my friends are seekers and we're on a growth journey together.

Friendship Pain Points

Even if you know your friendship values and have some great friendships in your life, no relationship is always smooth sailing. Friends hurt one another's feelings and create bad relationship habits all the time, but we're often not sure how to address it.

In our families, the occasional argument or misunderstanding is just part of how close relationships work, but in our friendships, we sometimes have this misconception that we should let things go or not cause drama. Over time, this adds up to resentments and sometimes even full-blown friendship breakups over things that could have been dealt with much earlier.

Here are the pain points that seem to come up over and over again when I talk about friendship online:

I'm Lonely Even Though I Have Friends

What does "lonely" mean to you? You don't have enough on your social calendar? You don't feel seen and known by your friends? You have friends, but they rarely check in or initiate casual interactions? It all feels more effortful than it should?

Figuring out which version of lonely you're feeling will help with the solution. Sometimes it's a case of seeking out new friends, either because it's nice to have a variety or because your current friends aren't the right fit. Your loneliness might be a hint to start initiating the interactions you want. Reach out to others with more frequency, or set up a social gathering.

As an introvert myself, I'm not going to pretend those actions are breezy. It might take everything you have to plan and execute a friend date. But no one is going to pull you out of your own loneliness. You're going to have to take some action.

There's a Money Imbalance

The older we get, the more complicated the money thing is. At all levels of income, this still feels like the great unspoken in many relationships. Transparency about your financial situation might help the logistical piece, but the awkwardness remains, and I've heard many stories about how money was a major factor in friend groups splitting or individual relationships drifting apart.

If a friendship revolves around activities that cost money, like meals out or trips or shopping, it makes sense that it would become a strain on those with tight budgets. In a perfect world, times of connection shouldn't be dependent on spending money, and good friends would be at least loosely aware of one another's limits. But we often hide our financial woes, or we assume that everyone else is as comfortable spending or saving money as we are, and the lack of communication can get ugly fast.

Whatever you do, stay mindful of this in your friendships. Remember, the thing about money is that anyone's situation can change at any time. Wherever you fall on the financial spectrum, withhold judgment on your friends' spending habits, be generous when you're able, and make plans that feel right for everyone.

Why Am I Always the Initiator?

This is the most common complaint I hear about friendship across the board. Those who feel like they're always the ones reaching out, always the ones planning the next gathering, are tired and frustrated. And their feelings are hurt.

I personally can't relate to this, because it's not typically the role I play in my friendships. In fact, hearing so much hurt and exhaustion from people online over the years has made me much more aware of how often I don't initiate things, and I've tried to be better about it.

An imbalanced friendship isn't fair. There has to be a certain level of give-and-take, of shared effort, not every single day but over time. The net benefit of friendship should be positive and as equal as humanly possible given all the factors at play, even if we're talking about years and not weeks. The simplest definition of a friend is someone who wants to spend time with you. While it can be toxic to keep score in a friendship, it can be equally toxic for one friend to bear the burden of holding a friendship together by keeping it going.

I do think there's a personality type at play here.

Extroverts and people who are skilled at planning or who keep up with the latest fun restaurants or who have more margin to call for a chat are going to get stuck being the initiators more often, and the rest of us will benefit from that (see: The Yes Friend). But I do have compassion for the constant initiators, and I've been in a friendship group where the usual social ringleader went on strike until someone else picked up the baton.

I wonder if we could possibly reframe this? If it's your gift to do the planning, I can guarantee that your friends appreciate you, even if they haven't expressed it specifically. I literally would not have gone on trips with friends or even to dinners out if someone else hadn't planned them. It's just not my nature to be the social initiator. I'm grateful for my friends who are, and I mean that. But I'm not going to take the reins next time, either, unless something is said.

Initiators have a choice: you can reframe your role as a positive and necessary one (who would ever get together if we didn't have an initiator or a Yes Friend among us?), or you can teach people how to treat you by occasionally stepping back from this role and asking others to step up to the plate.

I'm not suggesting playing games, just trying to shift a well-worn relationship pattern. Nothing changes if nothing changes, so if you really want the dynamic to shift, you will have to be the one to do it. I assure you that no passively-minded friend will change her ways without a wake-up call.

But don't lose friendships over this if you truly don't mind taking on this role. You've probably become the initiator in your friendships because you're good at it. Let them know if you feel it's imbalanced, but also try to see it as the strength that the rest of us do.

I Feel Like We're Drifting Apart.
How Do I Address It without Being Clingy?

We've all experienced the great friendship fade, when the weeks and months between connections grow longer and longer until you stop considering the other person part of your friendship circle. In a best-case scenario, this is natural and mutual. But sometimes one person fades faster than the other.

The friendship fade can be the most humane way to draw a relationship to a close, especially if the circumstances make drifting more plausible, like physical distance. But for good friends, or those you still run into regularly, the slow disappearance of a previously close relationship can be torture.

First of all, if you suspect a friendship is changing, it probably is. I've learned to listen to my intuition in all things, but especially in my relationships. Yes, our anxieties and insecurities can make it hard to discern when someone is really acting weird or if it's all in our head, but I believe we should err on the side of trusting our own judgment.

The only two things I can do when a friendship feels like it's sliding toward a fade is to let it go or confront it head-on. If it's not a Life Council level friend (or somewhere in that emotional vicinity), letting it go is a fair option, at least for the immediate season. Especially if it doesn't feel personal, like if one or both parties are enormously busy, in the midst of a life change, or seem to be immersed in another friend group or relationship. I can only hope we've built a foundation of affection that will let us swing back around into friendship in the future, or if not, at least simply retain warm feelings.

It's different when a good friend pulls away. This can feel terrible and worrisome and can bring out all our worst assumptions. Ultimately, it usually requires some sort of inquiry. I start with a softball: *Hey, I've noticed we haven't talked in a while, and I miss you! Everything okay? Can we grab a drink together this Friday? You've been on my mind, and I'd love to catch up and connect.*

I want to show her that this reaching out is a step beyond checking in. It's taking the temperature of our friendship. Suggesting a specific time to meet and hang out is better than being generic about getting together.

Her response will give me more information about whether my instincts are correct or not. If she calls back right away or otherwise makes it clear that she's just been busy and over-whelmed, I must choose to believe her. This points back to my friendship mantra to *believe the best* in one another. But if she's lukewarm or nonresponsive, then I definitely know something's up, which leads to a harder pitch: *Hi. I miss you, and I feel like something is up between us. Are we okay? I'd love to see you this weekend and talk it through. Are you available Saturday afternoon?*

Being so direct might not be your personality and might not fit every level of friendship, but I do believe being clear is better than second-guessing, making incorrect assumptions, or remaining so vague that the problem doesn't really resolve itself. Keep in mind that whenever a friendship fades, it creates space for a new friend (see: The Empty Chair).

How Do You Know When to Break Up with a Friend?

This is related to the point above, but it's worth mentioning in case you're the one who is fading first. If you are asking yourself this question, you already know the answer. Give your own intuition the credibility it deserves. If you're this far down the road of contemplating ending a friendship, something obviously isn't working.

So what now?

Do friendships need big, dramatic, official breakups? For the most part, they do not. Creating some distance and then a slow fade will suffice in most instances. Of course, if you're very close friends, then more explanation will probably be needed, and if there's been a betrayal or transgression of some kind, then a formal severance is warranted.

It can be incredibly hard to admit that you're trying to let a friendship fade to someone who is asking you directly. This can cause all kinds of drama you'd rather avoid. Still, author Brené Brown teaches us that being clear is kind. Being unclear is unkind. There are courteous ways to do this:

- *I'm stepping back a bit from our friendship because I'm not sure we're on the same page.*
- *I need a little space in our friendship for now.*
- *I feel like we're on different paths, and I really need to focus on my own.*

Fill in the gaps and details as necessary, sharing as much information that makes your intentions known without piling on the hurt. As I've already shared, I've been on both sides of a friendship ending, and it is never pleasant, even if it is necessary. Do your best to end friendships with everyone's integrity intact.

I Feel Left Out or Uninvited Because I'm Sober or Single or a Parent or My Life Just Looks Really Different from Yours

After complaints about always being the initiator, the next most common form of angst that fills my inbox when I talk about friendship online is feeling left out because someone's life has changed. Single friends want to continue to be invited to dinner after a friend gets married, and new parents want to be included even though their schedules are upended.

The details get lost in these stories because they're all remarkably similar: most of us want to stay connected even when our circumstances change the dynamic. The plea I hear so often is simply not to be forgotten. And not to make assumptions about whether or not I want to hang out based on some stereotype about my (or your) new life.

For the most part, no one is trying to hurt anyone else's feelings when our invitations change because of life circumstances changing. In fact, we might think we're doing a friend a favor by not subjecting them to a crying baby or a rowdy drinking party. But in my informal Instagram research, married people want to be included, single people want to be included, parents want to be included, those without kids want to be included, sober people want to be included—you get my drift. We just want to be a part of one another's lives. It's not that deep. Why do we make this harder than it is?

We are all just people. Not our labels. Not our relationship status. Let us try to love one another as individuals and not as stereotypes.

A Friendship Requirement

The good news is that despite all these pain points and angst over our friendships, there is really only one important requirement in our friendships: *presence.* A wise and kind friend taught me this when comforting my husband, who had just lost his brother Dave after several years battling cancer.

Dave was beloved by so many people, there was a wide circle of friends with whom we wanted to share about his passing in the hours immediately following, so we had a system in place to disseminate information when he died. My role was to call one of the men, a dear friend, who would then call the others. We used to call this a phone tree, a system that's been all but abolished with the many ways we now have of spreading information, but in times of crisis and pain, it's still surprisingly effective.

This friend I called had seen his own share of loss and pain, and when he saw my phone number on his screen, I'm sure he knew what would follow. After I choked out that we had lost Dave, I continued to sob into the phone. I asked this longtime friend of my husband's what I should do next. I was standing **YOUR PRESENCE IS ALL THAT'S REQUIRED.** on the porch, a summer breeze was blowing, and I had no idea what I was supposed to do when I hung up the phone. He answered: **your presence is all that's required.**

Over the next few hours, days, months, and years, my presence was the best thing I could offer.

It was a simple, powerful message, even though it felt strange to "only" be present, and not be ticking off to-do items. For the rest of the summer, when we retreated to our lake house for a season of quiet grief, simple presence became profound.

It seemed others had learned this lesson long before I did. At the lake, our local friends came to check on us every day. Sometimes they'd offer food or a boat ride, but most of the time they'd just stop by the dock and say hello. Check in. Chat for a moment and then head back home. Those quick visits when we were hurting meant everything to us.

In the years since then, I've reminded myself that my presence is all that's required when I stress about helping a friend through something. I debate if I should show up on their doorstep or give them some space. I worry if I should make freezer meals or send a grocery gift card. As soon as I start to wonder if I'm doing right by a friend in need, I remember that presence is all that's required, and the decision becomes easier. Even if the "presence" is sometimes just a text reminder that I am present.

By nature, "presence" might look different in the different friendships on the Life Council. A Daily Friend can step in and take over carpool. A Business Bestie could let you disappear into work and not talk about it. A New Friend might leave food on the porch. A Yes Friend might get you out of the house on the weekend. And an Old Friend lets you sob on the couch for as long as you need.

The work of being a good friend changes over the course of your life and in different relationships but the basics remain the same: consistently show you care, aim for good communication, and most of all, be the friend to others that you want for yourself.

Fostering a Culture of Healthy Friendships

We've spent the majority of this book focusing on our individual friendships, from those that already exist to those we hope to cultivate. But we can't forget the importance of fostering a culture of healthy friendships.

Our friendships feel personal and intimate to us, but all of our relationships are shaped in some way by the wider culture. If we want to turn the tide from an epidemic of loneliness, we have to pay attention to the broader topic of friendship in our communities and families.

By this, I mean we should be intentional about teaching our children about friendship, sharing specifics in our friendships, being honest about relationship trends and how they're affecting us, and staying aware of the general health of our own friendship groups.

Since we know that so many of our friendship lessons and habits are learned in childhood, it's up to each generation to teach the next how to do friendship better. Teaching our kids how to make friends and how to be a good friend will pay enormous dividends in their lives. When we learn as adults how to navigate complicated relationships and how to make an effort to maintain our friendships, we model behavior that our children will use over and over again. Periodically making new friends and frequently inviting others into our homes and lives teaches inclusion and vulnerability. All of this bodes well for a generation which also has to contend with the ever-changing landscape of modern relationships.

Friendship Groups

We can often judge the temperature of our immediate culture by the health of our friendship groups. The Life Council is comprised of individual relationships, but most of us are a part of a wider friendship group in one way or another, and the bigger the group, the more potential there is for drama and exclusivity. We would do well to pay attention, not just to our direct relationships, but to the larger dynamic at play. Do people feel like they belong? What are some of the common roles among group members? Is the door open or closed to outsiders, and, depending on the circumstances, does that make the group feel safe or stuck?

In your friendship groups, try to notice if someone has pulled back or if someone is leaning in, then inquire about what's going on. Pay attention if someone grows extra quiet at dinner or on the text thread or if there's a dominating person-ality that affects the equilibrium of everyone else.

Navigating different group dynamics could be a full-time job if we let it, so don't take these suggestions as further chores for your relationship to-do list, just keep it in the back of your mind next time you're out together or the reply-all emails are flying around. Participation in our friend groups is part of the bigger conversation of our lifetime of friendships and will play a part in how we think about our own Life Councils, our most trusted advisory group.

On Boundaries

The wave of self-care and self-advocacy advice online has had some very positive effects on mental health awareness and erasing the stigma of therapies and personal improvement, but I've seen some negative consequences as well. Deeming other people "toxic" has become so common that we're now applying the term to people we disagree with or with whom we have a conflict. Setting personal "boundaries" in our relationships is meant to protect our overall well-being and can be a good and necessary thing, but I have to wonder if we've boundaried ourselves all the way into loneliness. There is a tipping point where you can have so many boundaries around your time, your environment, and your interactions that you've constructed a world that keeps other people out instead of inviting them in.

HAVE WE BOUNDARIED OURSELVES ALL THE WAY INTO LONELINESS?

Relationships are never perfect because people are flawed. In our friendships, we have to accept that there will be a certain amount of imperfections, including disagreements, misunderstandings, awkward moments, and flat-out mistakes. If you set the standards so high for your relationships that people are constantly disappointing you, you'll probably struggle to connect. One of the best parts of friendship is that we can be ourselves around one another, and if you give it enough time, those selves become the best version possible of us because we were seen and loved in the context of a fulfilling friendship. When you wall yourself off, you miss all of that.

Sharing Specifics

In my first book *Share Your Stuff. I'll Go First.*, I was all about sharing yourself in order to build connection with others. I've been preaching about the power of sharing for years now, and there's one thing I've come to believe that is very important in the context of our closest friendships: you must share specifics about your life with your trusted friends.

We've been conditioned to protect our spouses and children and institutions at all costs, which means that when most of us are asked about hard seasons we're walking through, we distill our struggles down to vague phrases, such as:

- *Our marriage is in a bit of a rough patch.*
- *Parenthood is the hardest thing I've ever done.*
- *This job will be the death of me.*
- *My childhood wasn't great, but it's all in the past.*

We gloss over what's really happening, sometimes even to ourselves. We definitely don't share the details of what we're calling "hard." We're too embarrassed. Or, we've been taught that to say anything bad about our family or job or community to outsiders is being disloyal. But when we keep the details of these difficult things a secret, we lose all discernment (if we ever had it) of what is a "normal" amount of struggle in our relationships or what has tipped over into unhealthy, even abusive, behavior.

For example, when we're told that "marriage is hard," some of us take that to mean that verbal abuse or manipulation is par for the course. We think being miserable in our marriages is just a regular part of partnership. Isn't that why there are so many jokes about how tough marriage is?

But if you were to share specifics of what was said in a fight or who slammed the door or who walked away or who took the first step to make up, what would a trusted friend say? Would they nod and maybe share a story of a similar argument in their relationship? Would they be able to offer solidarity? Or would they gently suggest counseling or something more? Maybe they would try to explain to you that what you're describing feels a bit more serious? So many women get too far down the road in their struggles without seeking help or a solution because they carry the burden alone, without sharing the specifics with anyone who can see the situation more objectively. A Life Council-level friend will point you towards a path of growth because they want what's best for you.

I understand the resistance to sharing specifics. In the beginning of our struggles, it's just easier to keep them inside. We're hopeful they'll simply pass, or we don't want anyone prying apart our sensitive spots. But when we speak aloud about exactly what's happening, it lets us face it. And when we do this with a friend, we don't have to face it alone. Drop the idea that sharing specifics is disloyal to your partner or family or boss. Keeping secrets usually only serves those who are exerting power over someone else. Step into your own power by refusing to stay silent when things are hard.

Our closest friends can be mirrors. When we share

ourselves, they reflect our words or actions back to us. Sometimes this lets us see more clearly what we're saying and feeling, and it may snap us back to reality after a long spell of denial. It also gives our friends permission to be honest about what's happening in their lives, and this exchange of vulnerability takes our relationships deeper.

One caveat: Please do take care if and when you decide to share specifics about a struggle in your life. Make sure it's with a trusted and thoughtful friend. I don't think it's something many of us would approach casually, but the rewards for this kind of sharing and knowing one another are invaluable, and it could change your life.

Keep Friendship a Priority

Making friends and nurturing our friendships is a lot to navigate, especially if we're not used to putting such a focus on these relationships and have relied on them continuing passively instead of actively. But I can't think of anything more important than our care for one another. This goes way beyond our individual Life Councils. This is a chance to make friendship the priority it deserves to be.

HOW WE SHOW UP PUBLICLY AND PRIVATELY IN ALL OUR FRIENDSHIPS IMPACTS OUR BROADER COMMUNITIES.

For me, fostering a culture of healthy friendship looks like refusing to participate in unkind group dynamics, gossip, or purposeful exclusion. It looks like talking to my kids about what it takes to choose our friends and modeling being a good friend. It looks like highlighting voices and resources who are tackling the wider friendship topic.

How we show up publicly and privately in all our friend-ships impacts our broader communities with a ripple effect of care and consideration for others. Kindness is contagious. Generosity of spirit spreads through our connections. And there is nothing needed more than these things right now.

CONCLUSION

You Don't Need a Busload of Besties

As I was working on this book, our family moved across town, and my daughter started a new school. For the first time in many years, I was in a situation where I was meeting new people and gauging our friendship chemistry while also trying to put my best self forward in every interaction. It was both exhilarating and exhausting.

Even as someone who makes a living talking about connection, I had my share of stumbles in conversations and awkward encounters. I cared if I was dressed "right," I noticed if I was or wasn't invited to something. I sent more than a few handfuls of tentative, new-friend texts with suggestions to get together. Sometimes these were reciprocated and sometimes not. I tried not to take any of it personally, because I've been the busy one who forgets to reply to the new acquaintance.

I'm always open to making new friends, but I was also

painfully aware of the slow friendship fades happening in other areas. Life was shifting, and it was uncomfortable.

So I made myself stay mindful in the process of these relationship transitions. I said yes to the invitations I received, even if they were sometimes inconvenient. I tried to be a good conversationalist and ask people questions about themselves. I reminded myself that putting in the effort to make new friends was an investment that pays dividends for years. I did my best to keep an open heart, with an eye on that Empty Chair that awaits a possible friend.

We learn about making friends when we're very young, but we're not taught much about keeping them (or releasing them, for that matter). Most of us don't even think that deeply about the state of our friendships until we're forced to confront it after a time of hurt or loneliness. But deeper examination often reveals that we're not all operating under the same ideas about these relationships, which furthers our isolation and confusion about how to have good friends during adulthood in a rapidly changing culture.

I wish that I had been more intentional about my friend-ships in the past, back when I thought friends were an unend-ing resource and I believed it would always feel natural to make them a priority. I couldn't conceive of a life so busy that I had to schedule time with friends weeks in advance, and I would have cringed at the idea that I'd still feel left out or hurt by friendship drama in my forties.

It took years of talking and writing about friendship before I realized that it's not a topic you grow out of. Women I know at every age, in all kinds of different life circumstances care about what's happening in their friendships as much as they care about their careers or marriages or anything else we deem important. We just don't talk about it as openly, and we lack guidance on how to foster the friendships we want.

If I could tell my younger self anything about friendship, it would be this:

> Pay attention to who you surround yourself with—attitude, energy, and kindness matters.
>
> Your friends will be one of the biggest influences of your entire life, so make sure you've chosen well.
>
> Be the type of friend to others that you've always wanted for yourself.
>
> Learn when to fight for a friendship and when to let go with love.

And finally:

You don't need a busload of besties. What you need is an assembly of friends throughout your life who offer different strengths and experiences. You need friends who can be advisors and companions, who will help in times of need and cheer you on in times of joy.

What you need is a Life Council.

Resources

Platonic by Marisa G. Franco (New York: Putnam, 2022).

All About Love by bell hooks (New York: William Morrow, 2000).

The Dance of Connection by Harriett Lerner (New York: HarperCollins, 2001).

Radical Compassion by Tara Brach (New York: Viking, 2019).

The Gifts of Imperfection by Brené Brown (Hazelden Publishing, 2010).

Adam Grant, "How to Make Friends, According to Science," *The Atlantic,* September 2018.

Acknowledgments

The Life Council as a concept is something I've unconsciously pursued for nearly forty years, and The Life Council as a book idea has been in the making for almost a decade. It started at a retreat while sitting in a circle of friends I'd met on the internet and was further solidified in a 2016 episode of the *Sorta Awesome* podcast I recorded with Meg Tietz titled "10 Friends Every Woman Needs," which then became the subtitle of this book.

It has been a dream to write about the women who have been my greatest influences and companions. They deserve all the credit for enduring years of relationship with me, as being friends with a neurotic, anxious, introverted person who is always threatening to write about you is probably a challenge. I hope I did all of our friendships justice.

Cara Pence has been one of my best friends since fifth grade, and she is still my first emergency phone call. Of all the words I spill everywhere, thank you for always hearing what I don't say.

Meg Tietz is the only person who fits nearly every seat on my Life Council, and her spirit is on every page of this book.

Thank you for letting me copycat you at every turn, starting at fifteen years old, and for the grace and wisdom you've shown over and over again, online and off.

Lindsay Lawler is my first and forever roommate, even though we haven't lived together for a long time. Thank you for getting every iteration of me over the years. There is no one else who makes me laugh harder without saying a single word.

Kimi Dallman and I are no longer mistaken for twins, but Kimi, you will always feel like a sister to me. Thank you for a friendship that transcends our worlds. I promise to pick up every time you call.

Jaime Hammer was my first friend crush and features in so many of my favorite and formative memories. Thank you for being a bright light in every room. Everything changes, yet somehow, we stay the same.

Julie Stillwell, Patty Chavez-Joy, and Tracy Herriott transformed my mom friend circle in a matter of weeks back in 2016. Our years of being happy pals together gave me the courage to tackle the friendship topic publicly, even when I felt like a fraud. Thank you for always cheering me on and trusting me to tell our stories well. Being with you feels like who I am now.

Amber Haines makes me want to love poetry and dig in the dirt; she's the one who taught me to marry the spiritual and the earth. Chris Ann Brekhus inspires every table I set with her ability to create beauty with whatever she finds in the nearest drawer or pulls from the closest shelf. Thank you, ladies, for bearing witness to my friendship journey, and for being the representatives in this book of a friendship group that is so meaningful. I just had to say it somewhere.

Jennifer Welsh is one of the only people who met me that

first year in Los Angeles and stuck around to see all that happened next. Thank you for becoming part of our family, Welshie. I'd rather be friends than coworkers. Speaking of that first year in LA, thank you to Megan Bell Bouchareb for holding me through 2001 and 2002. It was the most important year of my life, and I'm so glad we did it together. Extra special thanks to Cyndi Finkle, who tucked us under her wing but also expected us to fly.

Jamie Golden has spent so many hours dissecting every little thing with me over the last few years that she holds two Life Council seats in this book. Thank you for making me smarter about my business and my pop culture commentary. It matters.

Kendra Adachi and Bri McKoy are the other half of the business mastermind that led to me launching a podcast and writing books. Along with Jamie, they all kept straight faces the first time we held a business mastermind meeting over Zoom, and I promptly burst into tears when it was my turn to share. Why they're really getting the gratitude here, though, is because I've cried in almost every single meeting since then. Thank you, friends, for listening to all of my words and trusting that I would figure it out. We are a council unto ourselves.

Jenna Fischer is featured as a New Friend in this book because becoming friends with her was a turning point in my friendship life, but at this point, our beautiful relationship can no longer be considered new. Thank you for all the little ways you've taught me how to connect, even from just across town.

These friends have a presence sprinkled throughout the book, directly or indirectly, and I am so grateful for their roles in my life: Sarah Bessey, Yasmin Dunn, Andy Duty, Rick

Kosick, Lauren Mourer, Shauna Niequist, Ryen Pollock, and Nish Weiseth.

Though this book focuses on just a dozen or so of the closest friendships of my lifetime, there are so many other special relationships woven through these stories. I hold these friends and our memories close to my heart: Ashleigh Baker, Joy Bennett, Katie Cantey, Megan Cobb, Ashley Denton, Lora Lynn Fanning, Abby Fraser, Kelly Gordon, Michael Gretza, Jen Johnson, Emily Jones, Leigh Kramer, Elizabeth Liu, Shanna Newton, Allison Olfelt, Kristin Potler, Morgan Shanahan, and Katie Soter.

I could not have written this book without Caroline Klobas and Colleen Powell, the team that takes all of my ideas and musings and makes them happen. I am also indebted to friends who have given me advice and insight for years: Kristen Howerton, Emily P. Freeman, Rebekah Hoffer, and Retha Nicole. I am especially grateful to David Gate for letting me use his poem to open the book and for writing poetry that speaks straight to my soul.

Thank you to my agent, Lisa Jackson, and my editor, Carolyn McCready, for believing in this book long before I did, and enormous thanks to Angela Scheff, who spent long months helping me shape all of my ideas around the Life Council concept into this project. Thank you to the entire Zondervan team who enthusiastically supported taking *The Life Council* to the next level: Alicia Kasen, Harmony Harkema, Matt Bray, Sarah Falter, and Paul Fisher.

Finally, thank you to my husband, Jeff, who saw firsthand the effects of a lonely friendship season and encouraged me to find my people. And to our incredible children, Lucy and Finch, who know no other life than this one we've created together—it is bigger than my biggest dreams. If y'all need me, I'll be upstairs in the closet, hunkered over my desk or wrapped around a microphone.

I dedicated this book to those friends who have served on my longtime Life Council. We are who all those songs, movies, and books are about.

Discussion Guide

The Life Council: 10 Friends Every Woman Needs is perfect for book clubs and group discussions among friends and colleagues.

Here are a few questions to guide these conversations:

Part I:
The Most Important Relationship

How do you feel about deeming friendship the "most important relationship" in our lives?

What did you learn about friendship when you were young? Have those ideas served you in adulthood, or do they need reexamination?

Share a story about a friendship from your childhood.

Try to recall a time when you were hurt by a friend and ask yourself if that experience shaped the friendships that followed.

What have your friendships looked like in the past few years? What relationships are fulfilling, and what areas feel lonely?

Do you have any friendship philosophies?

> Reminder that my five friendship philosophies are:
> Friendship Is a To-Do
> Believe the Best
> Just Go
> Like Every Selfie
> Your Spouse Is Not Your Best Friend

Did you have a strong reaction (positive or negative) to any of the friendship philosophies I shared?

Part II: The Life Council

Does the idea of having a Life Council resonate with you?

Which of the Life Council members were you able to easily identify in your life?

Which of the Life Council members do you feel you lack?

Which of the Life Council members do you think you are on your friends' Life Councils?

Is there a position you would add or delete from the Life Council I've described?

Part III:
What I've Learned About . . .

When is the last time you made a new friend?

Have you ever made a friend online or in an unconventional way?

Do you feel more connected in friendship groups, or do you prefer one on one relationships?

What are your friendship pain points?

What advice would you give to your younger self about friendship?

How can you be a good friend and foster healthy friendships going forward?

For more resources, go to www.TheLifeCouncilBook.com.

Share Your Stuff.
I'll Go First.

10 Questions to Take Your Friendships to the Next Level

Laura Tremaine

Part memoir and part guidebook, *Share Your Stuff. I'll Go First.* is the invitation you've been waiting for to show up with your whole self and discover the intimate, meaningful friendships you long for. In spite of the hyper-connected culture we live in today, women still feel shamed for oversharing and being publicly vulnerable. And no matter how many friends we seem to have, many of us are still desperately lonely. Laura Tremaine, blogger and podcaster behind *10 Things To Tell You*, says it's time for something better. Openness and vulnerability are the foundation for human growth and healthy relationships, and it all starts when we share our stuff, the nitty-gritty daily details about ourselves with others. Laura has led the way in her personal life with her popu-lar blog and podcast, and now with lighthearted self-awareness, a sensitivity to the important things in life, and compelling storytell-ing, Laura gives you the tools to build and deepen the conversa-tions happening in your life. Laura's stories about her childhood, her complicated shifts in faith and friendships, and her marriage to a Hollywood movie director will prompt you to identify the beautiful narrative and pivotal milestones of your own life. Each chapter offers intriguing and reflective questions that will reveal unique details and stories you've never thought to tell and will guide you into cultivating the authentic connection with others that only comes from sharing yourself. So let's get started! Share Your Stuff. I'll Go First.

Available in stores and online!